Literacy Learning for Infants, Toddlers, & Preschoolers

Key Practices for Educators

Tanya S. Wright
Michigan State University

Sonia Q. Cabell
Florida State University

Nell K. Duke
University of Michigan

Mariana Souto-Manning
Erikson Institute

National Association for the Education of Young Children
Washington, DC

naeyc®

National Association for the Education of Young Children

1401 H Street NW, Suite 600
Washington, DC 20005
202-232-8777 • 800-424-2460
NAEYC.org

NAEYC Books
Senior Director, Publishing & Content Development
Susan Friedman

Director, Books
Dana Battaglia

Senior Editor
Holly Bohart

Editor II
Rossella Procopio

Senior Creative Design Manager
Charity Coleman

Senior Creative Design Specialist
Gillian Frank

Publishing Business Operations Manager
Francine Markowitz

The text in the "Concepts of Pictures" section on page 42 is adapted, with permission, from N.K. Duke, R.R. Norman, K.L. Roberts, N.M. Martin, J.A. Knight, P.M. Morsink, & S.L. Calkins, "Beyond Concepts of Print: Development of Concepts of Graphics in Text, Pre-K to Grade 3," *Research in the Teaching of English* 48 (November 2013), 175–203.

Figure 3.2 on page 75 is reprinted, with permission, from The Great First Eight Curriculum (GreatFirstEight.org), 2022, Regents of the University of Michigan.

Table 5.2 on page 124 is reprinted, with permission, from Bank Street. Adapted by the National Center on Culturally and Linguistically Responsiveness from N. González, L.C. Moll, & C. Amanti, eds., *Funds of Knowledge: Theorizing Practices in Households, Communities, and Classrooms* (Mahwah, NJ: Erlbaum, 2005).

Figure 5.4 on page 127 is printed, with permission, from "Berry Itchy Day," *Molly of Denali* (WGBH Boston).

Photo Credits

Copyright © Getty Images: cover (all except top left), 13 (bottom), 37, 57, 61, 80, 87 (top), and 111

Courtesy of the authors: cover (top left), 5, 11, 13 (top left and top right), 87 (bottom), 88 (all), 90 (both), 91 (all), 92 (all), 93, 94, 100, 101, 102, 103 (both), 108, and 123 (both)

Printed in the United States of America.

Library of Congress Control Number: 2022933542

ISBN: 978-1-952331-08-4

Item: 1161

We dedicate this book to teachers of young children. Thank you for all of the work that you do!

Tanya, Sonia, Nell, and Mariana

Contents

About the Authors

Tanya S. Wright, PhD, is associate professor of literacy in the Department of Teacher Education at Michigan State University. She earned her PhD from the University of Michigan. Dr. Wright is a former kindergarten teacher whose research and teaching focus on literacy instruction during the early childhood years. She is the author of several books for teachers, including *A Teacher's Guide to Vocabulary Development Across the Day*. Dr. Wright is lead author of *SOLID Start*, an open-access science and disciplinary literacy curriculum for grades K–2 (http://solidstart.msu.edu). She is senior editor of *The Reading Teacher*, a peer-reviewed journal that publishes research-based practices for literacy educators working with children up to age 12. Dr. Wright received the International Literacy Association's Jerry Johns Outstanding Teacher Educator in Reading Award in 2022. Follow her on Twitter @TanyaSWright.

Sonia Q. Cabell, PhD, is associate professor of reading education in the School of Teacher Education and the Florida Center for Reading Research at Florida State University. Before receiving her PhD at the University of Virginia, she worked as a second grade teacher and literacy coach. Dr. Cabell's research focuses on early literacy instruction with a particular interest in the prevention of reading difficulties. She has authored over 60 publications, including research articles, books, book chapters, and early childhood language and literacy curricula. She has served as principal investigator or co-principal investigator on federally funded research projects totaling approximately $9 million. Dr. Cabell has been an advisor or consultant for a variety of national organizations and state departments of education. Follow her on Twitter @SoniaCabell.

Nell K. Duke, EdD, is professor in literacy, language, and culture in the School of Education and the combined program in education and psychology at the University of Michigan. As of September 2022, Dr. Duke serves as the executive director of the Center for Early Literacy Success at Stand for Children (www.stand.org). She earned her bachelor's degree from Swarthmore College and her master's and doctoral degrees from Harvard University. Her work focuses on early literacy development, particularly among children living in economic poverty. Dr. Duke has received the International Literacy Association's William S. Gray Citation of Merit for outstanding contributions to research, theory, practice, and policy. Her website is www.nellkduke.org. Follow her on Twitter @nellkduke.

Mariana Souto-Manning, PhD, is the fifth president of Erikson Institute in Chicago. She has served as professor of education at Teachers College, Columbia University, and held academic appointments at the University of Iceland and King's College London. Committed to the pursuit of justice in early childhood teaching and teacher education, Dr. Souto-Manning's research (re)centers methodologies and pedagogies on the lives, values, and experiences of intersectionally minoritized people of color. As she problematizes issues of colonization, assimilation, and oppression in schooling and society, Dr. Souto-Manning critically examines theoretical and methodological issues and dilemmas of doing research with communities of color, considering questions such as "Critical for whom?" and "According to whom?" Dr. Souto-Manning authored and coauthored 10 books, dozens of book chapters, and over 80 peer-reviewed articles. She has received a number of research awards, including the American Educational Research Association Division K Innovations in Research on Diversity in Teacher Education Award. Follow her on Twitter @soutomanning.

Introduction and How to Use this Book

Have you ever watched an infant babbling away as you read to them? Have you listened to a toddler as they chant along with a favorite book? Or helped a preschooler by writing words that they dictate to you? From infants' curiosity about books to preschoolers' growing understanding that spoken words are represented by text on a page, young children are literacy learners!

Literacy learning begins at birth and continues throughout our lives. Young children's early language and literacy knowledge and skills build a critical foundation for their later success in reading and writing. We might see an infant learn to say the exact words that adults read again and again in a favorite book, a toddler scribbling on paper to "write" a birthday card, or a preschooler acting out a favorite story in dramatic play. We should support and encourage these moments because young children are learning about how reading and writing work.

Early childhood educators play a critical role in supporting young children's early literacy development. The specific practices that support literacy development in early childhood are sometimes different from those used by educators who serve older children. We want to support young children's literacy learning in ways that make sense for their age. The goal is to create learning opportunities for young children that build a foundation for reading and writing.

In this book, we focus specifically on the ways that early childhood educators can help to foster young children's literacy development from birth to age 5. NAEYC has been—and continues to be—committed to supporting early childhood educators in this work. We explain the latest research on supporting early literacy for infants, toddlers, and preschoolers and how early childhood educators can implement these practices with young children. Because play and playfulness are mainstays of early childhood education and have enormous potential to develop literacy, in each chapter we include examples of the power of play to support the aspect of literacy development featured in that chapter.

Five Critical Areas for Young Children's Literacy Development

We focus on five important areas for young children's language and literacy development, one in each chapter.

Chapter 1: Clever Communicators. Both language and knowledge are critical for understanding texts and for learning about the world. In Chapter 1, early childhood educators learn to support young children in building knowledge and in developing language, including vocabulary, to talk about the concepts they learn and texts that are read.

Chapter 2: Print Navigators. As children interact with different types of written text, they learn about how print is used to convey meaning. In Chapter 2, early childhood educators learn to support children's print awareness and understandings about print through intentional teaching and by encouraging children to engage with literacy materials in meaningful ways.

Chapter 3: Sound–Letter Linkers. The understanding that oral language can be broken into smaller sounds is a critical building block for literacy development. Understanding the relationship between these sounds and the letters we use to represent sounds in named languages (such as English or Spanish) is foundational for both reading and writing. In this chapter, early childhood educators learn to use games and activities that encourage children to play with sounds in words as well as developmentally appropriate ways to teach young children to recognize and associate letters with common sounds.

Chapter 4: Resourceful Writers. In the early childhood years, children can begin to represent their ideas using pictures, symbols, and eventually letters. In Chapter 4, early childhood educators learn to encourage and support children's attempts to share their ideas through writing.

Chapter 5: Text Comprehenders. Young children can understand, enjoy, learn from, and apply ideas from texts and images. In Chapter 5, early childhood teachers learn to engage children in read alouds and other interactions with written text that facilitate text comprehension and higher-order discussion.

Key Practices for Early Childhood Educators

Within each chapter, we discuss eight key practices for early childhood educators:

- Knowing
- Showing
- Designing
- Including
- Engaging
- Explaining
- Observing
- Responding

These practices enable educators to support young children's literacy development. While in the everyday world of the classroom, all of these practices are interrelated, but for purposes of this book, we've paired key practices for discussion in each chapter. The key practices are color-coded within the text of the book.

Knowing and Showing

Knowing. Early childhood educators need specific professional knowledge to help them effectively offer literacy-rich environments and experiences and respond to children's interactions within them. In this section of each chapter, we build professional knowledge, such as why the letter *w* is so tough for young children and how children's writing develops over time.

Showing. Young children learn so much by watching others. In this section of each chapter, we explain how to model specific practices for children, from modeling for infants and toddlers how to handle a book to modeling for preschoolers how to compose text.

Designing and Including

Designing. Planning for children's early literacy experiences is critical in the early childhood classroom. In this section of each chapter, we offer examples of how early childhood educators can design learning opportunities to foster children's literacy development.

Including. Part of enacting our ethical principles as early childhood educators is to strive to create an inclusive community at all times. This involves working to bridge and incorporate children's experiences in their homes and communities into their experiences in care settings or school. In this section of each chapter, we discuss ways we can include children, whether by selecting texts for read alouds that reflect children's cultural backgrounds or by building on children's interests when designing literacy-enriched dramatic play centers.

Engaging and Explaining

Engaging. A key aspect of fostering early literacy development is inviting children into interactions with written text and sustaining their engagement. In this section of each chapter, we suggest strategies for inviting and engaging children, such as literacy materials to include in the classroom environment and techniques for maintaining children's attention during read alouds.

Explaining. There are many moments in early literacy education in which explicitly teaching children what you want them to learn is the most effective and efficient move for an educator. In this section of each chapter, we provide guidance about when and how to explain ideas to children, offering sample teacher language for readers to consider.

Observing and Responding

Observing. Early childhood educators will be most effective in developing children's literacy when they engage in careful observation of children's play and their interactions with oral and written language. In this section of each chapter, we suggest foci for observation that can be used in that area of development.

Responding. There is perhaps no practice more important for an early childhood educator than responding to the children in their care. In this section of each chapter, we identify specific ways to respond to children's literacy interactions, such as the extension and elaboration of oral language or helping children to represent the sounds they hear in words when they have ideas they want to share in print.

Throughout the book, we use features and sidebars to highlight some important points and practices. These include

- **Key Idea.** Includes important concepts that are essential to understanding the chapter topics and provides "takeaways" that capture some big priorities.
- **Recommended Resources.** Lists books, articles, and digital resources recommended by the authors for use in the classroom.
- **Research Note.** Highlights an important concept or idea that is supported by research; covers new research that makes us rethink what has been assumed or suggests a need to shift practices from the past.
- **Teaching Tip.** Provides ideas or activities that can be easily incorporated into the classroom.
- **Technology Tip.** Offers suggestions for appropriately integrating technology into play and learning.
- **Transitions.** Supplies ideas for using classroom transitions, such as putting on jackets for outdoor play, as opportunities for literacy learning.

We encourage you to discuss these as well as the main body of the text with colleagues. Processing what you are reading with other professionals will help you enact more of the book's principles and practices.

Let's Learn More!

The time from birth to 5 years old is critical in building the foundation for early reading and writing. It is the responsibility of early childhood educators to make sure that children have daily opportunities to grow as literacy learners. You *can* support our young literacy learners in ways that are engaging, inclusive, and a lot of fun! We invite you to read on to learn more.

1

Clever Communicators

We are educators, authors, and researchers—and we are also mothers. Whether in classrooms or our own homes, young children have amazed us with their language and knowledge! One of my (coauthor Nell Duke's) favorite memories of my daughter's language development occurred in the bath section of a store. I looked away from my daughter, then a toddler, just for a moment. When I looked back, my daughter was holding what looked like a small pink ball (later revealed to be a bath bead). I asked, "What do you have there?" My daughter replied, "A choking hazard! Imma go choke on it!" and ran away. I'm happy to report that my daughter did not put the bath bead in her mouth. As I look back on this memory, I love the juxtaposition of the very sophisticated language she had picked up with the very toddler rebellion that followed!

Children make meaning of the world around them—the people, actions, and objects that they encounter every day. They categorize and make connections—between a loved one and closeness, between waving and departing, between a bath bead and a warning. Children read the world around them long before they read written texts. They use language to communicate with important people in their lives long before they read or write written texts.

Children read the world around them long before they read written texts.

KEY PRACTICES

Knowing and Showing

The key practice of **Knowing** is a starting point for supporting children's development as clever communicators. Knowing how children learn about language informs everything teachers do. **Showing,** another key practice, is the active response to Knowing. What we show children is based on what we know about their development and how to support them.

Knowing

Why are language and knowledge development so important in the early years? How can teachers support children's development in these critical domains?

In the early childhood years, children learn a lot about language and how it works. Children need to learn the meaning of many words so they can use their vocabulary to speak and listen. Children learn to combine words into phrases and sentences to communicate their ideas. They learn to understand the social aspects of language, including how to engage in a conversation with someone else. Children learn to understand that different people in their lives communicate differently and even draw from multiple languages that they know.

Language begins to develop before birth. Infants who are hearing recognize their parents' voices and use different sounds for different needs. As development progresses, infants attend to things that make sound and they babble and coo with regularity. They can take turns "talking" and interacting with family members and teachers long before they can use recognizable words. By about 12 months of age, infants may play simple games like peekaboo and can say one or two words, such as *papi* or *dada*.

During the toddler years (approximately 12 to 36 months), children begin to understand and use many new words. They begin to use two- to three-word sentences. Toddlers also follow one- to two-step directions. By the time children are preschoolers (ages 3 to 5), they use longer sentences to communicate and are able to understand—and be understood—in back-and-forth conversations with others. Preschoolers may use grammatical approximations as they develop their understanding of language. For example, a child might say, "I winned the game." Rather than correcting children's grammar, focus on encouraging children to communicate their ideas.

Children's language and knowledge also make a big impact on their reading and writing development. Readers need to be able to read the words in a book or other text, but they also need to understand what those words—and the text as a whole—mean. Readers need to understand the literal meaning of the text—what the written language means—and they also need to use their own knowledge to make inferences—filling in ideas that are not directly stated in order to reason about, learn from, and interpret the text. Likewise, a skilled writer can convey messages by using language for particular purposes. For example, writers use language to entertain, convey information, or share an opinion. For these reasons, children's language and knowledge also affect their reading and writing development. The language and knowledge needed to read for understanding and write for communication are critical aspects of early literacy development.

For example, early childhood teachers can help to support children's language and knowledge development when they

- Have authentic and responsive back-and-forth conversations with children
- Engage children in interactive read alouds of books
- Support children's learning about the social and natural world

The Language of Texts

The language we use in everyday conversation differs from the language that is used in texts. Written language used in the texts children encounter, even those read aloud to them at the earliest ages, contains many rare words as well as more complex sentence constructions than when we speak (Hayes & Ahrens 1988). This is why it is important to expose children to a wide range of texts to share the language of books from many cultures and linguistic contexts.

Consider the following two sentences from *The Napping House,* by Audrey Wood, illustrated by Don Wood, a book for toddlers and preschoolers:

> Can it be? A wakeful flea on a slumbering mouse on a snoozing cat on a dozing dog on a dreaming child on a snoring granny on a cozy bed in a napping house, where everyone is sleeping.

These sentences contain words, such as *wakeful* and *slumbering,* that are unlikely to be used in everyday conversations. Also, the formal way that the sentences are written ("Can it be?") does not sound like the way people usually talk. And yet, with support from teachers and family members, children can still understand and enjoy *The Napping House* and other books that use complex language.

When young children are regularly exposed to written language found in texts, they develop an understanding of these different ways of using language.

Vocabulary

Learning the meanings of new words is a particularly important part of children's language and literacy development. Children must know words and their meanings for speaking and listening as well as for reading and writing. In the example from *The Napping House* above, children will have difficulty understanding the sentences in the text (and the story more broadly) if they do not understand the meaning of the word *wakeful.*

Vocabulary is important for comprehending text and for using oral and written language. The more words that children know, the more easily they can express their thinking and ideas in oral language and in their early writing. Children learn the words that are used in meaningful ways in their environments—in discussions, in read alouds, and when they learn new things. Early childhood educators must offer many opportunities for children to learn new word meanings across all parts of the day. These words should reflect children's multiple language practices across contexts and not be restricted to the language of school. For example, children may play with words, bringing two languages (such as Spanish and English) together to say *parkeando* instead of *parking* (English) or *estacionando* (Spanish). This is because multilingual children do not separate named languages from birth; instead, they draw on their full communicative resources to communicate. These remixes—also known as *translanguaging* (a term explained later in this chapter)—are a common part of the language development process for multilingual children and children growing up in multilingual communities.

Knowledge Development

As children learn more about the natural, social, and engineered world, they are better able to understand the ideas in texts. For example, when an author writes that "the sky is getting darker," children can use their knowledge about the natural world to understand what this means. Either the day is getting closer to nighttime or a storm will soon arrive. Both of these inferences require knowledge about the world that children learn and observe in the world around them during the early childhood years. The more children know about the world, the more they can use that knowledge to understand new texts and learn new language and ideas.

The more children know about the world, the more they can use that knowledge to understand new texts and learn new language and ideas.

Both language and knowledge are vital for understanding what we read, what is being read to us, or what we watch (such as television programs). We use language and knowledge not only to more fully comprehend texts but also to learn new ideas from engaging with texts. For example, when a child already understands that plants grow in the ground, a teacher can build on that understanding by reading aloud a book about what plants need to grow (for example, water and sunlight). The child gains both new knowledge and new vocabulary.

Language and Knowledge

As we learn new concepts and ideas, we need to learn the words associated with those ideas. For example, when children are growing plants, they need to learn many new words to talk about how plants grow. New words might include some parts of a plant (*seeds, roots, stems, leaves, bud, blossom, bloom*), some of what plants need (*sunlight, water*), and how plants grow (*bigger, taller, wider*).

Learning new words is important for infants and toddlers who are learning about the world around them. Early childhood educators can support learning in many ways. During meals, for example, the teacher can name the foods that children eat (*yogurt, banana, rice*). While taking a walk outside, the teacher can point out plants seen along the way (*flower, cactus, maple tree*). Such naming happens in contextualized ways and through authentic interactions.

Each time a child learns the meaning of a new word, teachers can help children to learn new concepts associated with that word. For example, as children learn about the word *friendship,* they might also learn about how to make new friends, treat friends kindly, and include new friends in their play.

RESEARCH NOTE

Learning Words in Meaningful Categories

Studies show that learning words in meaningful categories is helpful to children (Hadley et al. 2019; Neuman, Newman, & Dwyer 2011). For example, children can learn words for different types of fruit (*cantaloupe, mango, grapefruit*), words for different emotions (*upset, excited*), or words related to moving with our legs (*jump, run, stroll, hop, skip*). Teaching words in meaningful categories helps children make connections between words and concepts. For example, mango and cantaloupe are both types of fruit because they both grow on plants, have seeds, and can be eaten.

Children who are learning more than one language benefit from connecting word categories across languages. For example, a child who is learning Spanish and English may know two words for *cantaloupe,* one in each language; know that the word *mango* is the same in both languages; know the word *grapefruit* only in English; and know the word *guanábana* (soursop) only in Spanish. The child may recognize all of these as fruit and have the ability to communicate about fruit with speakers of more than one language. A multilingual child may use words from more than one named language in the same sentence (*translanguaging*). This is common to multilingual children who are talking with others who are also multilingual. The use of translanguaging—that is, drawing on a child's full communicative resources and crossing what adults label as named languages, such as Spanish or Swahili—does not mean that the children do not know the vocabulary in the other language; it simply means that they have more possible words to use to communicate. Instead of correcting the child, early childhood teachers can extend and deepen children's knowledge by asking questions, such as "What does guanábana mean?"

Showing

Children learn language throughout their day, both at school and at home with their families. When children are at school, teachers are language role models. Teachers show children every day how to use language to meet a variety of purposes. This section discusses some of the most effective ways to model language use with children and engage in conversations.

The Importance of Interactions

Young children's language grows through everyday interactions with others around them (Zimmerman et al. 2009). Early childhood educators play a critical role and can intentionally create opportunities to foster learning. The key is to be responsive to what children are doing and saying (Landry et al. 1997). Use children's actions and interests as starting points for conversations. Then, keep the conversation going back and forth on the same topic. This builds children's knowledge about the world around them and helps their language grow (Piasta et al. 2012). You can also engage in modeling by drawing on more than one language if you are bilingual or multilingual. This practice is important to communicate belonging to multilingual children.

Topic Variety

Teachers can talk about a variety of topics with children of all ages; these topics should attend to young children's interests and consider their cultural context at home, fostering home and community literacy practices (Souto-Manning & Yoon 2018). For infants, whatever captures their interest at any given moment is the perfect topic of conversation. Talk about what they can see (for example, a ceiling fan) and touch (such as a soft blanket). Also, be sure to talk about what you are doing, especially when it involves them ("I am going to pick you up and change your diaper"). Diapering, changing, and feeding present excellent opportunities to talk. Even infants who are not yet talking can have back-and-forth "conversations" with you with their coos and babbles.

Toddlers love to talk about the here and now. Whatever is going on in their world at that moment is a great topic of conversation. Oftentimes, only adults very close to the child can understand what children are saying, in part because the child's language is understood within the context of their personal experience. For example, a toddler might point at something and begin verbalizing. If an adult didn't know what they were pointing at or why, it might be hard to figure out what they were trying to say. Building close relationships with young children and observing them carefully help you better understand their communications.

TEACHING TIP

Decontextualized Language

Talking about ideas and concepts that take place outside the child's immediate time and place is called *decontextualized language.* Hearing and using decontextualized language is very important for children's language development (Davidson, Kline, & Snow 1986; Rowe 2013). This kind of language does not depend on children's immediate context or shared experiences.

Some ways to encourage children to talk beyond the here and now include the following:

- **Discuss explanations.** Talk about the connections between events or how things work ("Why do you think the grass is being mowed today?").
- **Engage in pretend talk.** Join along in children's pretend play (If children are pretending to be doctors you might say, "I am not feeling well today. How will you take care of me?").
- **Talk about past and future events.** Encourage children to talk about things that are not happening right now ("We are going to visit the new park next week. What do you think we will see there?").

As children grow older, early childhood educators can help develop their language by encouraging them to expand beyond the here and now and talk about things that already happened or things that will happen. For example, a teacher might say, "Tomorrow we will go to the zoo. What do you think you will see there?" Teachers can also provide explanations to children about how things work, such as "When you press this button, the vacuum cleaner turns on."

Build on Children's Curiosity

Children are naturally curious about the world around them. At around age 3 or 4, children often start asking *why* questions, such as "Why is the sky blue?" or "Why are you doing that?" This natural curiosity offers many opportunities to build language. Foster conversations with children about a variety of topics. For example, when children are riding tricycles on the playground, a child might suddenly ask, "What if we ride to the end of the earth?" This surprising question can lead to conversations about the earth. Perhaps you might use a globe to show children that the earth is spherical. This might lead to even more complex conversations about the earth and geography.

Provide New Experiences

Along with following children's interests, early childhood educators can help them develop new interests by creating experiences through field trips. Firsthand experiences in new environments provide opportunities to talk with children before, during, and after the field trips. Specifically, when talking about what is seen and learned before and after events occur, teachers are helping children use decontextualized language. Take, for example, a field trip to a recycling center to learn about how trash is sorted. In the classroom before the visit, the teacher can read texts about recycling and composting. During the visit, the teacher can respond to children's questions and comments. After the visit, the teacher can extend what children learned about composting by showing children how to compost the apple cores and orange peels from snack time in their classroom.

Figure 1.1. Children enjoy their time on a field trip.

Field Trip Ideas from A to Z

- Apple farm
- Bookstore
- Community center
- Diner
- Exercise area
- Fire station
- Grocery store
- Hospital or doctor's office
- Ice cream shop
- Jewelry store
- Kitchen supply store
- Library
- Museum
- Neighborhood walk
- Outdoor space (park, nature trail, field, pond)
- Post office
- Quack-quack (duck) pond
- Recycling center
- Studio (art, music)
- Theater
- U-pick farm
- Vehicle lot (city bus fleet, car lot)
- Water or splash park
- X marks the spot (treasure or scavenger hunt)
- Your own ideas—anywhere in your community you think will spark children's interests
- Zoo

Build and Extend Language

Children learn from the adult language teachers use every day. By building on what children say, teachers are modeling language in ways that extend children's learning. For example, if a child at a sand table says, "Look!" the teacher might respond by saying, "You built a sandcastle!" This provides children with words (*built, sandcastle*) for what they are trying to communicate. When early childhood educators are attentive, warm, and responsive to what children are saying, they show children that their ideas matter.

When teaching and caring for very young children, it's helpful to note that children don't need to speak out loud to carry on a conversation. From the time they are born, infants want to communicate. They respond to our voices, facial expressions, and affection. Early on, they can take turns interacting back and forth with us (Trevarthen 2018). For example, when a 6-week-old baby coos, an adult can acknowledge this coo by saying, "Well, hello to you" or "Buenos días, mi amor" in return and waiting expectantly for another coo. Responding to a child in this way signals that their efforts to vocalize can affect the people around them; this experience also lays the groundwork for children's ability to engage in conversation.

As babies grow into toddlers and learn to say words (for example, pointing at a truck and saying "tuk" or pointing at a bottle and saying "baba"), we can repeat their words back to them during conversations ("Yes, that's a truck!" or "Do you want your bottle?"). We can also talk aloud about what they are doing while they are playing ("You are building a tower with blocks").

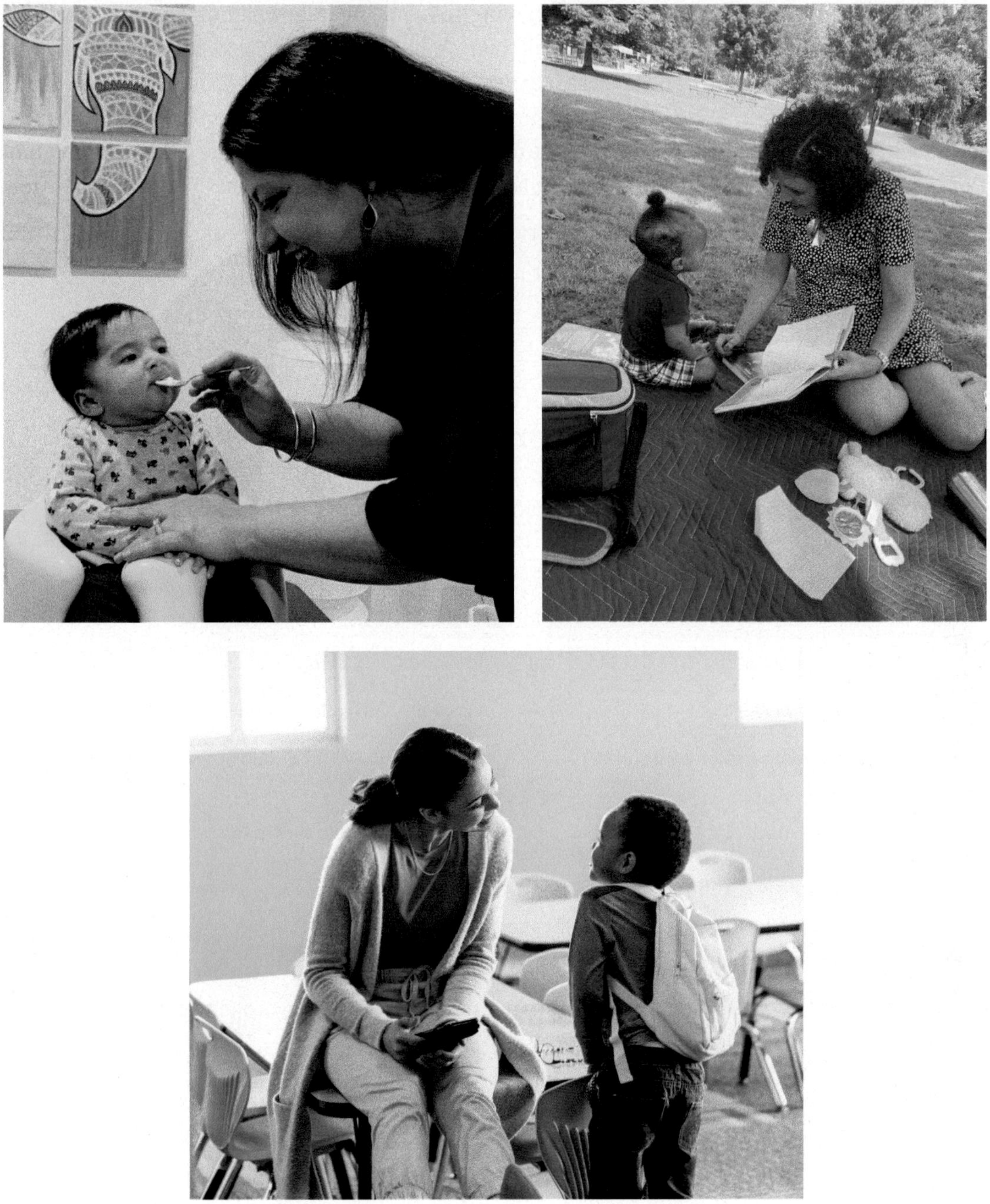

Figure 1.2. Communicating with young children at every stage of their development lays the groundwork for their ability to engage in conversation.

At 3 and 4 years of age, children can become more adept at carrying on conversations. They are developing the ability to take many turns in a back-and-forth conversation. To nurture children's language learning, keep the conversation going by asking open-ended questions. These are questions that don't have just one correct answer and that often require children to use more than one word to answer. Frequently these are questions that begin with *how* and *why*. Extend children's ideas by adding information to what they are saying. If a child says, "Baby is eating," respond by saying something like, "The baby is eating food so that she can grow until she is big and strong, just like you!"

The language of young children often does not sound like the language of adults. As children learn language, it is normal for them to speak with grammar that is invented, exploratory, or unconventional. Also, multilingual learners may use sentence structures that make sense in their native language (for example, "the chair blue" instead of "the blue chair"). Don't stop a conversation to correct children's grammar; instead, provide a language model and keep the conversation going (for example, "Yes, you are sitting in the blue chair"). This shows children that you value their ideas

TEACHING TIP

Ask Open-Ended Questions

Extend and expand conversations with children by asking open-ended questions.

Instead of asking . . .	Ask . . .
Are you reading a book?	What are you doing?
What color is the playdough?	What are you doing with the playdough?
Is your hot chocolate hot or cold?	How does your hot chocolate feel when you drink it?
Does Charlie feel mad?	Why does Charlie feel mad?

Table 1.1. Instead of Asking

To help children's language grow, consider the following strategies:

1. Repeat and reword what children say to expose them to advanced language models.

   Infant: Blue. (*Eats blueberries.*)
   Adult: Blueberries.

   Toddler: Sticky.
   Adult: That glue is sticky.

   Preschooler: I winned the game.
   Adult: Yes, you won the game!

2. Expand and extend what children say by adding an idea.

   Infant: Ka. (*Touches a cat.*)
   Adult: That's a soft cat.

   Toddler: Truck! (*Plays with a toy truck.*)
   Adult: Your truck is driving up the hill and down the hill.

   Preschooler: It's sunny today.
   Adult: It's sunny and the temperature is high; it's going to be very hot today.

and provides a model for learning. For example, if a child says, "Her is nice," respond by saying "Yes, she is nice." Or you might add a new word ("Yes, she is nice; she is kind") or an idea ("Yes, she is nice. Look at the toy she gave you!"). Try to keep the conversation going by asking an open-ended question, such as "What does she do that is nice?"

Knowing about young children's language development is critical for an early childhood educator. Showing children how to communicate by modeling with your own language—and through your responses to their language—is one of your most important roles.

KEY PRACTICES

Designing and Including

Designing as a key practice includes the intentional planning and preparation of the classroom, schedule, guided learning experiences, and materials to provide a rich variety of learning experiences. **Including** is a key practice essential to welcoming every child to the learning experience, ensuring equitable access to learning, and fostering respectful and affirming relationships.

Designing

Children's experiences hearing and using new language and learning new ideas matter. In early childhood settings, educators play an important role in bringing new words and ideas into the classroom. Learning may happen in spontaneous teachable moments, but educators must also plan and provide experiences, such as read alouds, explorations, investigations, and discussions. Educators must also plan and think about how to support children's language development during these experiences. Designing the learning experience is a key practice for supporting language learning.

For example, when working with infants, teachers can plan to use the words for people and objects in the child's environment. A teacher might name a toy when the child holds out their hand to ask for it (for example, "You want the rattle. Hold it in your hand. Shake, shake, shake!"). This encourages children's reactions and verbalizations. With toddlers, teachers can plan for more sustained exploration of topics, such as learning about parts of the body and how we use them (for example, a teacher might say, "You can walk on your feet, you can smell with your nose, you can smile with your mouth"). Preschoolers are excited to learn about all sorts of new topics through books and experiences inside and outside the classroom.

Questions Guide Planning

To purposefully design knowledge- and language-building opportunities, teachers need to have a plan. Questions teachers might use to frame their planning include the following:

1. What will children learn about over the next few weeks?
2. What experiences, explorations, and read alouds might help children learn these concepts?
3. What words and phrases can I teach children to help them to communicate about these new ideas?

The answers to these questions will vary depending on the setting. To determine topics and themes to focus on, consider the curriculum materials that you use, early childhood standards, and topics of interest to the children you work with.

For example, imagine a unit for toddlers on gardens and gardening. Here are brief responses to the previous questions:

1. What will children learn about over the next few weeks?
   - What gardens are, what grows in gardens, gardens in their community
   - Ways gardens can help people and animals (such as providing food)
   - Ways people and animals can help gardens
2. What experiences, explorations, and read alouds might help children learn these concepts?
   - Eating foods from gardens using family recipes, enjoying flowers from gardens
   - Exploring and observing gardens in the neighborhood and in videos
   - Reading books about planting gardens and plants and animals that live within them
3. What words and phrases can I teach children to help them to communicate about these new ideas?
   - Nouns, such as *seed, flower, fruit, vegetable, soil*
   - Verbs, such as *grow, dig, plant, cover, pick, water, peel*
   - Adjectives, such as *ripe, unripe, dry, moist, wet, colorful*

Plan for Participation

Beyond planning the content of the curriculum, teachers can also develop routines and practices that ensure all children will have opportunities to participate and share their thinking and ideas. For example, when reading aloud to children, the following strategies will help welcome participation:

- Keep a checklist to mark which children participated each day and encourage children who may not volunteer to participate.
- Read aloud with small groups of children so it is easier for all children to participate.
- Use think-pair-share. Children pause to think about a question or comment, pair with their "elbow buddy" (the child beside them), and then share their responses with one another.
- Include nonverbal opportunities for children to demonstrate their understanding, including signs or gestures that children can use to participate ("Give a thumbs up if you think . . ." or "Touch your nose if you think . . .").

Designing or selecting a curriculum and planning activities for language learning are key teaching practices necessary for supporting children's growth and development.

Including

All children's language attempts should be encouraged, including children who speak a range of home languages and dialects. The goal is to invite children's participation and to value children's ideas and experiences. For this to happen, educators need to ensure that children's different ways of communicating are fully and truly welcomed. Instead of focusing on including "other" languages, teachers need to work to learn from, honor, and sustain many ways of communicating.

Including all children in language learning is the responsibility of teachers. The goal, as stated in NAEYC's "Developmentally Appropriate Practice" position statement, is to "maximize language development," and to do that, "educators recognize differences in developmental progressions for monolingual, bilingual, and multilingual children and support the development of multilingualism" (NAEYC 2020, 26). To include all children in language learning, educators need to unlearn outdated information. For example, a few decades ago, there was a belief that children's language learning was limited and that learning many languages was confusing and overwhelming. This led educators to discourage young children's multilingual development, especially when there was concern about communication. They might even have told multilingual families to speak English at home. Today, the early childhood education field knows that this is not a valid concern nor valid advice. Families should speak in their most comfortable language(s) at home.

Multilingual Learning

Young children's communication is fluid and dynamic. Nevertheless, because multilingual children are making meaning and making sense *across* named languages, they may appear not to have as large a vocabulary. (Note: Here and throughout the book, when we say *multilingual*, we are referring to children who speak multiple languages and/or multiple dialects.) Further, children's words are not sorted by the names adults create for languages (for example, Spanish, English, Mandarin, second language). As young multilingual children communicate, they remix their sounds and words from across the languages they experience in their home, school, and community contexts. These flexible and creative uses of language need to be supported.

There are different ways that multilingual development has been explained throughout time. Some of the ways are explained in the Research Note that follows.

As young multilingual children communicate, they remix their sounds and words from across the languages they experience in their home, school, and community contexts. These flexible and creative uses of language need to be supported.

RESEARCH NOTE

Multilingual Development

The following are ideas about multilingual development that have evolved over time and are no longer seen as accurate or complete:

- **Language learning as separate and sequential:** the understanding that children sequentially acquire a first language (L1) and then a second language (L2)
- **Language interdependence:** the understanding that there are academic and linguistic transfers across languages
- **Code-switching:** the understanding that named languages exist separately and that children switch languages as we flip switches

While some of the earlier ideas are still present today, translanguaging reflects our most current understanding of multilingual development (García & Kleyn 2016). Translanguaging is the understanding that language is not organized according to adult-established labels for languages (named languages) but instead are blended together in one's linguistic repertoire (a language repository of sorts).

The Importance of Translanguaging

When early childhood educators enforce the separation of named languages, it inadvertently fosters exclusion, builds obstacles to communication, and upholds injustices in classrooms (Delavan, Freire, & Valdez 2021). Much of the research points toward the need to support young children's translanguaging. This translanguaging happens most commonly in the early years at the

- **Interword level,** which is when words that are typically categorized in different named languages are put together; for example, "More água, please!" and "Está raining."
- **Intraword level,** which is when, for example, the roots of a verb in one named language and the conjugation rules of another named language are blended together; for example, a child might say, "Look, I'm brincking!" In this example, the word *brincking* combines the root of the verb *brincar* (*play* in Portuguese) with *-ing* (a suffix to indicate present participle in English).

Educators need to be careful in their assessments of multilingual children. Partial and false cognates (words that have common elements across languages) can give a false sense of what young children know. For example, *embarazada* is the Spanish word for *pregnant*. An English speaker who wishes to say "I'm embarrassed" in Spanish might logically but mistakenly say "estoy embarazada," a comment that actually means "I'm pregnant."

Because this sophisticated knowledge about words often gets ignored or is misunderstood, it is important to support young multilingual learners in the classroom. There are some important ideas to consider to make sure that all children are supported in their language and knowledge

TEACHING TIP

Affirm All Language Systems

What is often referred to as African American English or Black English is as sophisticated and legitimate as any other language. Welcome and honor children's use of this language system as well as any of the ways of communicating children bring to the classroom.

development. These ideas, though, need educators to recognize that their own understandings of multilingualism must shift.

Support children's translanguaging to maximize communication and promote a positive sense of self and multilingual practices. As they share their ideas, children may speak using some words and ideas in their home language and some in the language spoken at school. The example below comes from Tara Lencl's toddler classroom in New York City and shows how monolingual teachers can encourage translanguaging, communicating the value of multilingualism.

> Martina, a 2-year-old Spanish-speaking child . . . is playing at the water table with a small group of children. Some of the children are standing on towels, but there's no towel at Martina's spot. When she realizes the floor is getting wet, the following conversation ensues:
>
> Martina: Necesito, necesito (I need . . . I need) . . . this one. (Pointing at the towel her friend was standing on.)
>
> Tara: Oh! You need a towel!
>
> Martina: Necesito towel.
>
> Tara: Here's a towel.
>
> Martina: Towel. (Spreading the towel on the floor and standing on it)
>
> (Genishi & Lencl 2015, 82)

To encourage children, value and respond to children's communicative attempts instead of correcting them. This is true of all of children's communications. A child who says, "I goed to the movies" should not be corrected. Instead, you might respond, "You went to the movies! What did you see?"

Strategies that Support Translanguaging

Strategy 1: Engage in translanguaging or make efforts to include translanguaging in your classroom. To illustrate the process of translanguaging and normalizing it in her classroom, Jessica Martell, a primary grade teacher in New York City, engaged in think alouds when authoring stories. For example, when telling a story about a big clean up, she wondered out loud, “Hmmm, uso trapear or mopear here? My setting is New York. Cual debo usar?” Another time, drawing on her Boricua identity, Jessica reasoned out loud, “If my story is en Puerto Rico, en la isla, debo escribir *chinas,* y no *naranjas,* porque no decimos naranja. Yeah, I should use *chinas* and not *naranjas.*” She explained that she must write the word *chinas* rather than *naranjas* because in Puerto Rico the term *chinas* is often used for *orange,* whereas in some other Spanish-speaking regions the term *naranja* is often used. This consideration of word choice and think aloud modeled the process of translanguaging.

Strategy 2: Include books that display translanguaging in the classroom and share them with families. Although not everyone translanguages, normalizing translanguaging means not only cultivating and sustaining young children’s translanguaging but also playing music that uses translanguaging in the lyrics, reading books (and have family members record audio of books) that feature translanguaging in writing, and having books that display translanguaging in your own classroom. Some examples are *Just a Minute: A Trickster Tale and Counting Book, Niño Wrestles the World,* and *Just In Case: A Trickster Tale and Spanish Alphabet Book* (all by Yuyi Morales). Other examples include *What Can You Do with a Paleta?* and *What Can You Do with a Rebozo?,* both by Carmen Tafolla.

Strategy 3: Counter resistance. Multilingual children may resist translanguaging. This is because even at ages 3 and 4, they may have come to internalize various aspects of linguicism. *Linguicism* is when people or systems discriminate against people based on their language use. For example, in the United States, people who speak with a southern dialect have often been discriminated against in newscasting positions. One type of linguicism that children and families may experience is linguistic racism—when ways of speaking associated with the racially dominant group are seen as a norm or valued over other ways of speaking and when ways of speaking of marginalized groups are deemed inferior and discriminated against (Baker-Bell 2020). Linguistic racism can be particularly harmful because it occurs alongside other forms of racism. As early childhood educators, it is so important to recognize and reckon with the fact that it is likely some children and their families have received the message that their ways of communicating are inferior, broken, or need fixing. Educators must work toward linguistic justice through valuing all children and families’ language use.

Strategy 4: Learn more about multilingual children’s language. Often, children’s ideas and words may not be familiar to teachers. In a young toddler classroom, for example, coauthor Mariana Souto-Manning’s 1-year-old son engaged in translanguaging, using the word *água* for water and *vovó* for grandmother. When Mariana first met her son’s teacher, the teacher asked Mariana to record and write down 10 words that were key to his communication and what they meant. This was the beginning of a process of partnership between Mariana and her son’s teacher, who expanded her knowledge of Portuguese as she taught Mariana’s son, valuing his contributions and validating his communicative efforts. As teachers, it is important to learn terms that children use to communicate. This not only facilitates attachment and connection but also communicates to all children that teachers are language learners too. Mariana’s son’s teacher demonstrated translanguaging as she inserted keywords in her communication, deepening her connection with Mariana’s son. This offers lessons for all teachers to honor young children who are multilingual.

. . . teachers are language learners too.

Strategy 5: Include opportunities for children to learn from family practices, knowledge, and experiences. To include families as partners in the education of young children, engage in a mapping (taking stock) of the expertise shared across the families and communities to which the children you teach belong. In Eileen Blanco and Lisa Wilson's kindergarten classroom, 4- and 5-year-old children were asked to interview a family member about the history of their names to contribute to a class book on the topic. Jessica Martell asked family members to visit her classroom and share with the children some of the skills they use at home and work. For example, to expose children to the importance of accuracy in procedural texts (such as recipes, instructions, and manuals), she invited one child's mother, who sold tamales for a living and spoke Spanish, to share with the children how to make tamales. From this mother's visit, the children learned about language and built new knowledge. And when children were intrigued by how the broken window in the very tall One World Center Building would be replaced, Jessica asked a parent to talk about harnesses, hazards, and safety measures for construction workers, again extending children's vocabulary as well as their knowledge (Souto-Manning & Martell 2017). This allowed for the experiences of the children's families to inform the learning in the classroom.

Strategy 6: Make the community your classroom. Much of what exists in the community surrounding your early learning setting is likely to serve as a source of valuable learning experiences. For example, riding the city bus, watching birds, and going to author talks and read alouds in bookstores are some examples. In a toddler classroom, the construction work happening outside its window became an opportunity for learning. Toddlers interviewed one child's father, a construction worker. In a preschool classroom, a visit to the natural history museum led to the transformation of the sand table into a paleontology station, where children could dig for dinosaur bones. The paleontology station included large and small chisels, magnifying glasses, small toy geological hammers, brushes, trowels, notebooks, and pencils. This activity eventually led to the development of a guide to dinosaurs with characteristics, names, and more.

Strategy 7: Teach children language for respectful disagreement. To foster respect and understanding, engage children in respectfully disagreeing. One way of doing so is by modeling disagreements starting with *I*. Teachers can model this by saying, "I hear you say that *papai* sounds like *popeye*. Lucas calls his dad *papai*. It is *daddy* in Portuguese." This avoids accusations and provides opportunities for learning about each other's language, family, and more.

Strategy 8: Value children's ideas through classroom inquiry. When you don't understand children's ideas, sometimes the easiest and most immediate action is to dismiss them or to change the topic. To foster learning about and through language, those partly understood or not-at-all understood ideas can become the center of an inquiry-driven learning process. This means that when a child brings up, for example, La Llorona (The Weeping Woman, who instills fear in young children to behave), instead of dismissing it as not relevant or—problematically—as folklore, the class can engage in learning more about this part of Mexican Indigenous oral traditions and its significance to many Mexicans, Mexican Americans, Latinxs, and Latin Americans (Souto-Manning, Ghim, & Madu 2021).

Engaging and Explaining

Engaging children in conversation is a key practice that happens throughout the day during planned activities, daily routines, and play. Through the key teaching practice of **Explaining,** teachers provide supports for language learning.

Engaging

Conversations invite children to engage in learning and build their language and knowledge. Conversational interactions can take place all day—during whole group discussions and read alouds, small group time, indoor and outdoor play, mealtimes, and transitions. Intentionally inviting children to enter into conversation about interesting topics is key to supporting language development.

Use a Variety of Engaging Texts

Teachers can introduce different types of texts to engage young children. These might include informational texts, storybooks, rhyming books, and digital or audio texts. Digital texts from trusted sources (for example, www.pbskids.org) that are designed for preschoolers are an appropriate tool for engagement and learning in preschool classrooms. Audio texts, such as songs, audiobooks, and podcasts for preschoolers, also have a place in preschool classrooms.

Use Informational Texts

Informational texts are especially good for learning new content because their primary purpose is to teach or inform. For example, a book designed to teach children about fish is an informational text, whereas a story designed to entertain children through the adventures of a fish is not. We say *texts* rather than *books* because books are not the only valuable material for young children. Magazines, online articles written for young children, nature videos, and other materials can also be informative and interesting to young children.

Inspire Curiosity

Human beings are curious by nature. Even young infants actively explore the world around them and, as they become more mobile, their explorations expand. Early childhood educators can build on children's curiosity and exploration to facilitate their language learning. For example, you can encourage learning in infants by placing an interesting object out of reach, such as a toy that the baby hasn't seen recently. The infant will need to "ask" for that object. An infant may babble or use words to refer to that object. This creates an opportunity for a back-and-forth conversation, where the adult repeats the child's vocalizations or narrates what they are reaching for ("You want the toy elephant, don't you?").

RECOMMENDED RESOURCES

Magazines for Young Children

- *Babybug*
- *Click*
- *Highlights Hello*
- *Highlights: High Five*
- *Highlights: High Five Bilingüe*
- *Ladybug*
- *National Geographic Little Kids*
- *Ranger Rick Jr.*
- *Zoobies*
- *Zootles*

As children move into toddlerhood and then preschool, expose children to new topics and ideas. Children's curiosity motivates them to learn new things. For example, we recently heard a 4-year-old from Florida, where it rarely snows, ask, "What does snow become when it grows up?" Adults can respond to such questions by saying, "I'm wondering if what you want to know is where snow comes from and what happens to snow when it goes away." This can lead to a conversation and read aloud introducing ideas about the water cycle.

Here are a few more ideas for introducing new ideas and concepts. These strategies invite children to take an active role in exploration and learning:

› **Add a new object:** Place a new object in the classroom, such as an interesting (and safe) kitchen tool, a piece of natural material, or an unusual or novel object (such as an old telephone). It won't take children long to start exploring and asking questions.

› **Model curiosity:** Demonstrate your own interest, and children's interest will soon follow. For example, when out on the playground, study a natural object, such as a leaf, or while at the sensory table, express your curiosity about what would happen if you put one cup inside the other.

› **Provide a sneak preview:** Show and tell children about a new book and then leave the book out on display. You may find that children later bring you the book with a request to read it.

› **Get out into the community:** Taking children out into the community—to the bakery, the lumber yard, or a local garden—will inspire children's curiosity to learn and connect new concepts.

› **Study a topic in depth:** You may have heard the expression, "The more you know, the more you don't know." There is truth in this even for young children. Digging deeply into a topic (like in the unit on gardens and gardening described above) will lead children to generate new questions.

TRANSITIONS

Facilitating Language During Transitions

Transitioning between activities can be a meaningful time for talk. Facilitating language learning during transitions is another key practice. The following are just a few examples of the many ways you can support language development during transitions.

Infants: Changing a diaper is a great time to talk with infants. Let the child know what you are going to do ("Let's change your diaper!") and then describe what will happen ("First, I'm going to take your dirty diaper off and put it in the trash can"). If the child is holding a toy during cleanup, you might talk about where it should go ("Let's save your toy in this basket").

Toddlers: Try engaging toddlers in conversation while dressing them to go outside. You might label the clothes that you are putting on them and talk about their function (hat, gloves). You might ask them what they think the weather is like or talk about what they will do outside.

Preschoolers: Mealtimes are a wonderful time to encourage conversation among children. Many preschool centers have family-style meals, when children are facing each other while eating and serving food from passable bowls or containers. Try to encourage children to use decontextualized language and talk about things happening in their lives at home. To do this, children can tell stories of events that have happened or may happen ("What did you do yesterday?," "What are you going to do after school today?," or "What will you do over the weekend?"). You can also invite informative talk where children can share information they know with each other ("Let's talk about all the things we've learned about gardens!").

Use Play to Prompt Conversation

Play is the perfect opportunity to join children and invite them to engage in conversations that enhance language development. Play is also a good time to facilitate conversations between children and their peers as well as between teachers and children.

Infants: Infants can engage with teachers in playing simple games that foster language development. For example, a game of peekaboo encourages conversational turn-taking. When infants dump baskets of toys, teachers can talk about what they are doing and the kinds of toys that are all over the floor; for example, you might name each toy as you put it back into the basket ("You put the ball in the basket"). If an infant reaches for a spoon at lunch time, you might respond by saying, "You want the spoon." As the infant uses the spoon, you might say, "You are using the spoon to help you eat. Yum!"

Toddlers: Dramatic play encourages children to imagine and talk in more sophisticated ways. Teachers can play an active role. If a toddler is pretending to sell items at a bakery, you might pretend to purchase the items and have a conversation about what you are buying. The discussion could include words that describe the taste, texture, and price of different items; when you eat them; and why you like them.

Change the materials in classroom play centers frequently. Changing a basket of props from boxes of food to items used in a doctor's office offers children opportunities to learn and use new vocabulary. Offer many options for centers—a doctor's office, a restaurant, a bodega, the zoo, a garden, a grocery store, a flower shop, an ice cream store, a fire station. Changing play props encourages children to talk with you and their peers about a broad range of topics.

Preschoolers: Around ages 3 and 4, children's play becomes more complex. Keep conversations going by asking open-ended questions that encourage children to respond with more than just one word. If children are pretending to be veterinarians who care for animals, ask and model open-ended questions in the role of the doctor ("Tell me about your pet") and as the pet owner ("What kinds of services do you offer here? What is wrong with my dog?"). Asking *why* questions can encourage more complex thinking ("Why do I need to take my dog to the veterinarian?" or "Why does my dog need medicine?").

Help Children Talk to Each Other

Social interactions between children also play a role in language development (Justice et al. 2011). Infants can be encouraged to interact with one another when playing with objects around them. For example, you might roll a ball between infants and repeat their vocalizations.

Toddlers often engage in parallel play, playing side by side but not necessarily together. Encourage language by narrating what they are doing ("Shelby is shoveling sand into her big yellow bucket. Marcus is making a sand castle").

Play gives 3- and 4-year-old children many opportunities to practice language with their peers. Children at this age begin interacting more cooperatively with one another as part of their play. Early childhood educators can help children have meaningful conversations with each other by modeling language and encouraging interactions. If a child approaches you with a request, such as help putting together a puzzle, you can encourage them to ask a classmate ("Omar likes puzzles. Why don't you ask him to help you?"). If two children are playing together in a dramatic play center, you can encourage conversation by commenting on what they are doing ("You are cleaning and putting away the dishes") and suggesting ways they can play together ("I wonder whether you can work together to make a grocery list").

Foster Conversations

Teachers can intentionally facilitate situations that foster peer-to-peer interactions by modeling social conversations in front of children. A teacher may say to a child, "Kenzie is writing. Let's ask her about her writing." The teacher can model for both children how to ask the question, "Kenzie, can you tell me about your writing?" The teacher and two children can then engage in a back-and-forth conversation. Over time, children will initiate these conversations more frequently without teacher support. Learning language for social interactions is a process that involves both language and social skills. Keep an eye out for children who need help starting conversations. For example, some children with well-developed language may feel shy and need support engaging with peers.

TEACHING TIP

Conversation Starters

Here are some sentence starters you can use or teach the children to use to get conversations going:

- I like . . .
- I wonder . . .
- Can I help you with . . . ?
- You are . . . (describe what someone is doing)
- What are you doing?
- Can you help me with . . . ?
- Tell me about . . .

You can also start conversations by inquiring into photos and objects children bring from home:

- Who's this? What are they doing?
- What's this? Whose is it?

Finally, you may draw on children's curiosity to start a conversation:

- Guess what?
- I am very excited about something!

Explaining

Explaining words and concepts is one of the most powerful practices early childhood educators can use to support language learning for young children. Research suggests that children who experience more explanations are more successful in developing language and knowledge than those who experience fewer explanations (Weizman & Snow 2001). When we explain or show children (through words, images, or demonstrations) what a word or concept is, we help them to learn to use new words and understand new ideas.

Explain Words and Concepts

Explanations of words and concepts can happen in any part of the school day. Whether outdoors, at meals, or at play, teachers have many opportunities to explain words and concepts. Good explanations for children tend to be brief and relevant, and they build on what children already know. "Relate the new to the known" is common advice. Verbal explanations are not enough to convey the meaning of new words or concepts, especially with infants and toddlers. Whenever possible, use actual objects, photos, videos, movement, or other supports to help explain words or concepts.

For example, if introducing the word *spatula,* you might first bring in some spatulas for children to see and use in preparing snacks or for dramatic play. Giving children an object that they can see, touch, hold, and use will lend meaning to the word. When explaining a new word to children, use simple language. For example, when explaining the word *spatula* to children, you would not say, "It's a kitchen utensil designed to separate food from a surface as batter from a bowl or egg from a pan." There are too many unfamiliar words in this explanation, and the sentence construction is too long and complicated for young children. Rather, you might say, "This is a spatula. A spatula is a tool you can use in the kitchen. It can help you pick up or move food." This child-friendly explanation contains words and sentence constructions that children are more likely to understand. Explaining words and concepts in more than one way is also helpful because children have a variety of experiences—what is familiar to some children may be new to others.

A child-friendly explanation provides information that helps children make connections to other knowledge. For example, the explanation of the spatula provides information about the category that a spatula fits within (that is, tools you use in the kitchen). Studies suggest that providing information related to categories will benefit young children's word learning (Kaefer & Neuman 2013) as children connect this new word with other words they already know.

Build Language and Knowledge Through Read Alouds

Young children learn new words and concepts when adults read aloud to them (National Early Literacy Panel 2008). Read alouds are a fantastic way to introduce new language and concepts to a child because read-aloud texts contain words and ideas that may not be part of our everyday conversations. During read alouds, teachers can help children build language and knowledge by explaining words and concepts that children may not know, particularly if those words and concepts are important for supporting children's understanding of the meaning of the text.

Explain word meanings during read alouds. When reading picture books aloud to infants, you can point to pictures and say the word (*giraffe* or *truck*) or you can say the words and ask the infant to point to the picture ("Touch the giraffe"). Look for books with large, high-contrast pictures that are easy for infants to see.

Invite young toddlers to point to the pictures in the book. Then, in response, describe what you see. For example, "I notice that you're touching the *balloon*. Yes. That's a *balloon*." Older toddlers may join in and repeat words or phrases from the picture book ("Poor kitten" or "Good night, moon").

Preschoolers love to listen to stories and learn about favorite topics from informational texts. Read-aloud texts for preschoolers can include more print on each page and can introduce more sophisticated new words. Early childhood educators should preview the read-aloud book and plan words to teach. When a new word is used in the text, stop and briefly explain word meanings to children. For example, when reading the book, *Baby Polar Bears,* by Marie Elizabeth Salzmann, after reading the text, "Baby polar bears are born in dens," explain that a *den* is "a home for a large wild animal." You might add that "bears, wolves, and lion homes are all called *dens*."

After the read aloud, encourage preschoolers to say the new word. This helps children remember the word. Use pictures, props, movement, and examples to deepen understanding of word meanings. For example, you could show some pictures of other animal dens. Encourage children to use new words later in discussion and in their play. For instance, when children are outdoors and pretending that the space under the jungle gym is their home, you can say, "Your home reminds me of the polar bears in their *den*."

Encourage children to interact with the text. As young children talk about books, they practice using language. Read alouds should encourage children to interact with the teacher and what the teacher is reading; they should not just be a performance by the teacher. Teachers can support children's language development by encouraging children to participate too. For infants, revisit favorite pictures in a book. When the infant looks or points at a particular page or picture, provide words, movements, and sounds to supplement the text ("The duck goes quack" or "That's a yellow flower").

Young toddlers can begin to actively participate in read alouds by saying the words from familiar texts, particularly when books have a pattern or phrase that repeats (for example, "Brown Bear, Brown Bear, What do you see?"). Older toddlers like to answer open-ended questions, such as "What do you think is happening in this picture?" They can also make up their own versions of familiar texts. For example, children can change the words to *Brown Bear, Brown Bear, What Do You See?* by Bill Martin Jr., illustrated by Eric Carle, to make the text about the friends in their classroom ("Sara, Sara, who do you see? I see Maribel looking at me").

Preschool teachers can support children's language use by asking children to retell or act out favorite stories and by asking open-ended questions that allow for many different responses. For informational texts, teachers can ask, "What did you learn from reading this book?"

Learn more about interactive read alouds and selecting texts to read with young children in Chapter 5.

Help children to deepen word and world knowledge. Build children's language and develop their knowledge about the world by reading aloud from a set of books on the same topic. Reading a set of related texts provides an opportunity to revisit words and ideas, and allows children to connect information from one text to another. Teachers can use books to build on children's existing knowledge as well as to provide opportunities to encounter new experiences that may not be part of their daily lives. For example, children in Michigan can learn about whales by reading about them in a book or children can learn about the experiences of people from other cultures or with different life experiences.

Combining books and real experiences deepens young children's knowledge. For example, if toddlers enjoy playing with cars and trucks, you could read aloud from several books about vehicles and transportation, such as *Little Taco Truck,* by Tanya Valentine, illustrated by Jorge Martin. A trip to the construction site that children pass on the way to school can help them to connect the ideas in texts to their everyday experiences.

As preschoolers are learning about emotions, read aloud from books that focus on emotions, such as *La Catrina: Emotions/Emociones,* by Patty Rodriguez and Ariana Stein, illustrated by Citlali Reyes, as well as discuss the emotions that children experience throughout the day.

As you read, help children to make connections across texts. For example, you might help children to notice categories of words and information, such as the words for types of vehicles, types of emotions, types of cooking utensils, or parts of a plant. Explain how words and concepts relate to one another and how new words build on children's existing knowledge:

- "We already read that trucks and cars are vehicles. Today we are going to read about trains, which are a different type of vehicle."
- "You have been on the subway, which is one kind of train, but a freight train is another kind of train. A freight train carries things that people need from one place to another."
- "When people pay a driver to take them from one place to another, the car they go in is often called a *cab* or a *taxi.*"

Revisit new words at other times of the day. Children rarely learn a word or concept with one exposure. It often takes many exposures for deep learning. Using sticky notes, a clipboard, or other tools, keep track of words and concepts you introduce to children so that you can revisit them often. Include props, tools, and books in play areas to encourage children to use new words and ideas in their play.

KEY PRACTICES

Observing and Responding

Observing children is a key practice that informs our understanding of children's language learning—where they are now in their development and what they are ready to learn next. What we learn through observation will guide us in effectively **Responding** to children in ways that support learning.

Observing

Observing is a way to learn what children already know and can do. Observation informs how teachers support children's language development. Language development is one of the most important things to watch and listen for as you teach and care for children. Educators observe to understand how to foster the next steps in children's language development. They also observe to notice any language-learning difficulties. Early intervention for language difficulties makes a big difference for children!

Observing and Listening to Language

When should educators worry about children's language development? The American Speech-Language-Hearing Association (ASHA, n.d.) suggests consulting a speech and language specialist when you notice signs of language problems or delays. A list of major milestones and concerns are provided in the table that follows. However, note that it is important to observe for these milestones in the context of the child's linguistic practices. For example, a child who has met a development milestone in the context of the named language(s) used in their home (for example, Haitian Creole) does not have to meet that milestone in the context of the language(s) used in the learning setting. This should not raise concerns about a child's language development. Young children's language practices do not develop equally or at the same pace across contexts; many times, multilingual children may reach milestones (for example, vocabulary or inferences) in their home language earlier than in the language used in their learning setting. Nevertheless, it is important to understand a child's full linguistic development—within and across language practices. Depending on your own language facility, you may need to consult with families and colleagues to ascertain children's linguistic achievements in their home languages or in languages you may not be fluent in.

TEACHING TIP

View Multilingual Learning as an Asset

Note that multilingual children may show different patterns of language development because they are learning more than one language. Learning multiple named languages should not be considered a problem or concern. Yet, such a process is more complex. When young children are developing multilingually, they do not see the delineations of English and French, for example. Instead, they learn to separate terms, conventions, and practices via approximation, practice, and trial and error. Even if it takes longer to see and document the language of young multilingual children, never discourage multilingualism. In fact, teachers should encourage families' engagement in sustaining their children's multilingualism. After all, knowing more than one language is an important asset and strength for young children—and adults!

	Age	Milestones in Language Development*	Signs of Potential Concerns
Infants	By 3 months	• Recognizes voices of family members. • Becomes quiet or smiles when a family member talks. • Coos. • Cries differently for different needs.	• Does not smile at others in any context. • Does not interact or play with others in any context.
	By 6 months	• Attends to music and toys that make sound. • Looks in the direction of sounds. • Babbles and coos regularly.	• Does not babble in any context.
	By 1 year	• Responds to own name, familiar words, and phrases (these are context dependent, not generalizable. • Plays simple games like peekaboo. • Babbles in long strings ("mamamama"). • Waves bye-bye, shakes head. • Says one or two words ("dada").	• Makes a limited number of sounds. • Does not gesture to communicate (for example pointing, waving).
Toddlers	By 2 years	• Follows one-step directions (such as "Stop"). • Answers and asks simple questions. • Understands and uses many new words. • Uses two-word sentences.	• Has trouble understanding what others say in all settings (home, school, community) as visible in (the lack of) verbal and nonverbal responses. • Says only a few words or does not say any words by 15 months across home, school, and community settings. • Does not use two-word sentences by 2 years old across linguistic contexts (such as "Mommy, up!" or "Más agua, mamá!").

Table 1.2. Milestones* and Concerns in Language Development

Adapted from ASHA, n.d. For a more detailed account of language development milestones, see www.asha.org/public/speech/development/chart.

*Children may not achieve all milestones at the same time in all of their languages.

	Age	Milestones in Language Development*	Signs of Potential Concerns
Toddlers (continued)	By 3 years	• Follows two-step directions. • Understands and uses many new words. • Uses three-word sentences.	• Uses less than 50 words across contexts. • Has difficulty playing with other children across contexts. • Has difficulty talking with other children across contexts.
Preschoolers	By 5 years	• Uses four-word sentences and four sentences at a time to communicate. • Answers and asks when and how questions. • Able to have back-and-forth conversations with adults and other children. • Follows multistep directions.	• Continues to have difficulty playing and talking with other children. • Speech is difficult to understand by adults who don't know the child across settings. • Does not speak in full sentences across settings.

Table 1.2. Milestones* and Concerns in Language Development (continued)

Observing Knowledge

Besides observing children's language development, teachers also observe whether children are developing in their knowledge. As children learn about a new topic or theme, observe for the following:

- Do infants seem attentive when you point to and name objects in their environment in their familiar language? Do they look when you name things in a language familiar to them? (For example, when you say, "there's the light" or "olha alí, a luz," you want infants to turn and look at the light or para a luz.) For children growing up multilingually, ensure that observations are made across communicative contexts. (For example, talk to families to see if infants respond to familiar words and phrases in a language familiar to them at home.)
- Do toddlers and preschoolers include new ideas and concepts in their drawings or in their play? (For example, after a trip to the park, the children pretend to be the mommy and baby ducks that you saw.)
- Do children share ideas or comment when you discuss new things? (For example, children may run up to you and tell you that there are new leaves on the plant you are growing in the classroom.)
- Can preschoolers sort pictures or objects into categories (such as kitchen tools versus building tools)?

Responding

Responding to young children's language attempts is critical for supporting their language development. Particularly in a busy early childhood program, taking time to listen to and engage in conversation with children can feel difficult. Early childhood educators have to prioritize taking the time to encourage children to talk, acknowledging what children are communicating, responding attentively to what children say, and then encouraging them to say more. Responsive care and attention are essential for children's language development.

When you observe the child . . .	You may respond by . . .
Infants	
Looking at something, pointing at or reaching for an object, crawling toward something.	Saying the word for the object in the language that is most familiar to the child. "That's the light. You see the light."
Verbalizing (cooing or babbling).	Talking to the child or repeating the sounds that the child is making.
Attempting to say a word (child says "muh" for milk).	Being encouraging and saying the full word. "Bottle. You want your bottle."
Toddlers	
Saying two or three word phrases ("car go").*	Responding to the child by expanding on their phrase or idea. "Yes. That car is going really fast!"
Trying to say something but does not seem to know a word ("baby doggie").	Responding by validating the child's attempted language and providing the specific word or phrase. "That is a baby doggie. A baby dog is called a *puppy*."
Showing interest in a particular topic (for example, insects, dinosaurs, building tools, a favorite character).	Responding by finding and reading aloud texts that relate to the child's interest.
Preschoolers	
Still working on learning conventional academic grammar ("I goed to the park").	Rephrasing when you respond rather than correcting the child or telling them that they are wrong. "Yes. You went to the park after school."
Struggling to use language to support social interactions (the child grabs a toy, pushes a friend out of the way, or cries rather than asking for what they need).	Teaching language to support social interactions. "Do you want that toy? You can say, 'May I have a turn to play with that toy?'"
Looking at a book or "pretend" reading a book.	Supporting this behavior by offering books in different areas of the classroom and encouraging the child to tell you the story or information from each page. While doing so, ensure that you are aware of how books are handled in the context of the child's home (are the pages turned from right to left or from left to right?), which allows you not to make assumptions based on your own life, culture, and experience as the norm against which their behavior is to be measured.

Table 1.3. Observing and Responding

*Children may not achieve all milestones at the same time in all of their languages.

Moving Forward

Young children's ability to learn language and knowledge is astounding. Teachers enable that ability to flourish when they

- **Know** how young children's language practices and knowledge develop and how adult educators can support that development.
- **Show** children how to communicate in many contexts by modeling varied language use.
- **Design** activities and lessons that introduce new words and concepts.
- **Include** children of all language backgrounds, respecting, responding to, and extending each child's communications.
- **Engage** children in extended conversations during transitions, play, and throughout the day.
- **Explain** words and concepts in child-friendly, contextualized ways during read alouds, investigations, and other experiences.
- **Observe** children's language development, seeking additional support for that development if needed.
- **Respond** to children's language by extending and encouraging conversations and curiosity.

When thinking about language and knowledge learning, you might think of children as master chefs cooking up delicious dishes. Even with a few ingredients they can make something delicious, but the more and varied ingredients educators provide through key teaching practices, the better the dishes children can make. Let's stock that pantry!

References

ASHA (American Speech-Language-Hearing Association). n.d. "Early Identification of Speech, Language, and Hearing Disorders." www.asha.org/public/early-identification-of-speech-language-and-hearing-disorders/#language.

Baker-Bell, A. 2020. *Linguistic Justice: Black Language, Literacy, Identity, and Pedagogy*. New York: Routledge.

Davidson, R.G., S.B. Kline, & C.E. Snow. 1986. "Definitions and Definite Noun Phrases: Indicators of Children's Decontextualized Language Skills." *Journal of Research in Childhood Education* 1 (1): 37–48.

Delavan, M.G., J.A. Freire, & V. Valdez. 2021. "The Intersectionality of Neoliberal Classing with Raciolinguistic Marginalization in State Dual Language Policy: A Call for Locally Crafted Programs." In *Bilingualism for All? Raciolinguistic Perspectives on Dual Language Education in the United States,* eds. N. Flores, A. Tseng, & N. Subtirelu, 26–42. Bristol, UK: Multilingual Matters.

García, O., & T. Kleyn, eds. 2016. *Translanguaging with Multilingual Students: Learning from Classroom Moments.* New York: Routledge.

Genishi, C., & T. Lencl. 2015. "'My Mommy Doesn't Speak English': Supporting Children as Emergent Bilinguals." In *Handbook of Early Childhood Teacher Education*, eds. L.J. Couse & S.L. Recchia, 273–87. New York: Routledge.

Hadley, E.B., D.K. Dickinson, K. Hirsh-Pasek, & R.M. Golinkoff. 2019. "Building Semantic Networks: The Impact of a Vocabulary Intervention on Preschoolers' Depth of Word Knowledge." *Reading Research Quarterly* 54 (1): 41–61.

Hayes, D., & M. Ahrens. 1988. "Vocabulary Simplification for Children: A Special Case of 'Motherese'?" *Journal of Child Language* 15 (2): 395–410.

Justice, L.M., Y. Petscher, C. Schatschneider, & A. Mashburn. 2011. "Peer Effects in Preschool Classrooms: Is Language Growth Associated with Their Classmates' Skills?" *Child Development* 82: 1768–77.

Kaefer, T., & S.B. Neuman. 2013. "A Bidirectional Relationship Between Conceptual Organization and Word Learning." *Child Development Research* 2013 (6): 1–8.

Landry, S.H., K.E. Smith, C.L. Miller-Loncar, & P.R. Swank. 1997. "Predicting Cognitive-Language and Social Growth Curves from Early Maternal Behaviors in Children at Varying Degrees of Biological Risk." *Developmental Psychology* 33 (6): 1040.

NAEYC. 2020. "Developmentally Appropriate Practice." Position statement. Washington, DC: NAEYC. www.naeyc.org/resources/position-statements/dap.

National Early Literacy Panel. 2008. *Developing Early Literacy: Report of the National Early Literacy Panel.* Washington, DC: National Center for Family Literacy.

Neuman, S.B., E.H. Newman, & J. Dwyer. 2011. "Educational Effects of a Vocabulary Intervention on Preschoolers' Word Knowledge and Conceptual Development: A Cluster-Randomized Trial." *Reading Research Quarterly* 46 (3): 249–72.

Piasta, S.B., L.M. Justice, S.Q. Cabell, A.K. Wiggins, K. Pence Turnbull, & S.M. Curenton. 2012. "Impact of Professional Development on Preschool Teachers' Conversational Responsivity and Children's Linguistic Productivity and Complexity." *Early Childhood Research Quarterly* 27: 387–400.

Rowe, M. 2013. "Decontextualized Language Input and Preschoolers' Vocabulary Development." *Seminars in Speech and Language* 34: 260–66.

Souto-Manning, M., H. Ghim, & N. Madu. 2021. "Toward Early Literacy as a Site of Belonging." *The Reading Teacher* 74 (5): 483–92.

Souto-Manning, M., J. Martell, A.Y. Pérez, & P. Pión. 2021. "Translanguaging as Norm: Rejecting Narrow and Restrictive Notions of Reading." *The Reading Teacher* 75 (3): 339–50.

Souto-Manning, M., & J. Martell 2017. "Committing to Culturally Relevant Literacy Teaching as an Everyday Practice: It's Critical!" *Language Arts* 94 (4): 252–56.

Souto-Manning, M., & H. Yoon. 2018. *Rethinking Early Literacies: Reading and Rewriting Worlds.* New York: Routledge.

Trevarthen, C. 2018. "Conversations with a Two-Month-Old." In *Parent-Infant Psychodynamics: Wild Things, Mirrors, and Ghosts,* ed. J. Raphael-Leff, 25–34. New York: Routledge.

Weizman, Z.O., & C.E. Snow. 2001. "Lexical Output as Related to Children's Vocabulary Acquisition: Effects of Sophisticated Exposure and Support for Meaning." *Developmental Psychology* 37 (2): 265–79.

Zimmerman, F.J., J. Gilkerson, J.A. Richards, D.A. Christakis, D. Xu, S. Gray, & U. Yapanel. 2009. "Teaching by Listening: The Importance of Adult-Child Conversations to Language Development." *Pediatrics* 124: 342–49.

2

Print Navigators

When my (coauthor Tanya Wright's) daughter was 7 months old, I noticed something interesting when she would sit on my lap as I read familiar books. Before I would turn each page, my daughter would lean way over to her right, sometimes almost toppling off my lap in the process.

> "Brown Bear, Brown Bear, What do you see? I see a red bird looking at me." (*Leans.*)
>
> "Red Bird, Red Bird, What do you see? I see a yellow duck looking at me." (*Leans.*)

I eventually figured out that even though she couldn't physically turn pages yet, she understood where to look to see the next page of a book. She was leaning to the right to see what came next as I turned the page. Of course, I quickly grabbed the video camera to capture this very first (and very funny) evidence that my infant knew something about how print works!

While many believe learning about reading and writing begins in elementary school, in reality children learn a lot before elementary school that builds the foundation for later literacy learning. For example, in the years before elementary school, children may learn

- The purpose of a book is for reading
- How to hold the book
- How to turn the pages

- Where to start reading
- How reading proceeds (in English, from left to right and top to bottom on a page)
- That the print on a page tells us the words to say
- And much more!

That knowledge is called *print concepts* (also referred to as *concepts of print*, *concepts about print*, and *print awareness*). In this chapter, we explain what print concepts are, why they are so important, and how you can develop them every day with the children in your care.

KEY PRACTICES

Knowing and Showing

The key practice of **Knowing** is a starting point for supporting children's development as print navigators. Knowing how children learn print concepts informs everything teachers do to support this area of development. **Showing**, another key practice, is the active response to Knowing.

Knowing

Print concepts are fundamental understandings about how print works. Children need to develop these understandings to lay the foundation for reading and writing (National Early Literacy Panel 2008). It might seem natural to you now, as a longtime reader and writer, but print concepts are not natural to young children. Children's understandings of print concepts grow through interactions with print, as adults or older children around them read books and point out print in the environment. Children first develop general understandings about how print works and then move to more specific understandings about print related to letters and words.

Children first develop general understandings about how print works and then move to more specific understandings about print related to letters and words.

Print Concepts

Print concepts include understanding the following:

1. Print represents language.
2. Print is organized in a specific way.
3. Print is made up of symbols that represent parts of language.

Print represents language. Print is what we read and write for a variety of purposes. When you read the word *bird* to a toddler, they don't think of it as a word at all but rather as a flying animal. In the early childhood years, children first learn that *bird* is the word we use in oral language to refer to some flying animals. Children then begin to realize that words we say aloud, like *bird*, can also be written down. This is part of beginning to understand print concepts.

Developing these insights takes time. Toddlers and preschoolers typically focus on pictures in books rather than print, in part because the pictures mean something to them and the print may not yet have meaning. If young children look at the print at all, often it is because the print is embedded in the illustrations—for example, *honey, mel,* or *miel* visible on a jar of honey (Justice, Pullen, & Pence 2008). As teachers read to children, they can draw children's attention to the print so that print becomes interesting and meaningful. Children begin to understand that both the print and illustrations provide the meaning of a text.

As children are exposed to different kinds of print in their environments (such as signs, maps, lists, and books), they begin to see that print can be used for many purposes. Children learn that people write for specific purposes—to inform, entertain, or persuade. Even very young children love to be authors, and you can see their understandings about print concepts through their early writing attempts. (See Chapter 4 for more about young children's early writing.)

Print is organized in a specific way. Depending on the language (such as English or Arabic), print is organized in specific ways. We read words on a page in a particular direction. In some named languages, such as English, Portuguese, and Spanish, for example, we read from left to right and from the top to the bottom on a page (more about directionality in other languages later in this chapter). Reading text in any language requires a language-specific understanding of the directionality of print in that language.

Directionality of print will not match children's understandings outside of a print context. For example, consider how we get from point A to point B when walking:

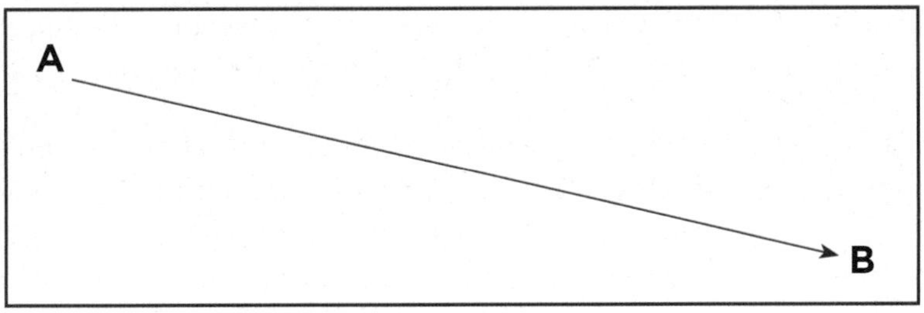

Figure 2.1. This is how a person would walk from A to B.

You would walk in a single, straight diagonal line. But consider how you get from point A to point B when reading print (see Figure 2.2).

Figure 2.2. When reading, you get from A to B very differently than when walking.

In addition, when readers get to the end of one line of print, they don't turn around and go back the other way on the next line, like a zigzag. Rather, when readers get to the end of one line, they pick up and start back at the beginning of the next line. This is called the *return sweep*, and it takes young children some time to understand that this is how we read print in languages like English, Portuguese, and Spanish.

Understanding print concepts also includes knowledge of how books are organized. Books have a "right side up," as well as a front and a back. There's a place in a text where we start reading. This place is typically not the copyright page, for example. It is often the page actually labeled with a numeral 1. Where we start reading may vary by the type of book and the situation. For some informational books, we might start by checking the index to find the information we need or looking at the table of contents by choosing a page to start reading.

Print is made up of symbols that represent parts of language. In English and many other languages, groups of letters make up words. An understanding that print is made up of symbols that represent parts of language is an important print concept. In addition to understanding the more general insights of print—that it represents language and carries meaning—young children begin to learn about letters (at least in alphabetic languages, such as English and Spanish) and words.

Children learn that the orientation of symbols matters a lot in print. The orientation of a symbol relates to how it is positioned on the page. The importance of orientation is something that must be learned. In most aspects of our lives, an object is an object no matter how you orient it. A teddy bear is still a teddy bear, for example, whether we turn it upside down or on its side. In contrast, with letters, the orientation of a letter can entirely change its identity:

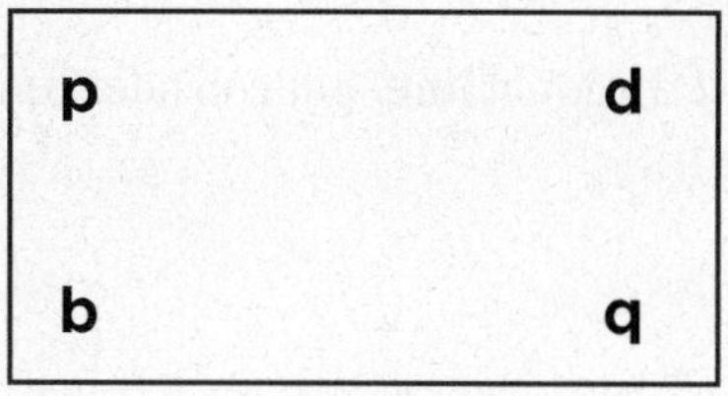

Figure 2.3. The orientation of a letter can change its identity.

These letters are the same shape, but orienting them differently changes what they mean. This is why you might see preschoolers write with letters oriented in different ways—backward or upside down. They are still learning this concept of print.

Another important print concept is that letters represent sounds. For example, the letter *n* makes the sound you hear at the beginning of the word: *no*—/n/. (In this book, when we talk about a sound, rather than a letter, we will place slash marks before and after the letter or letters that represent a sound.) The understanding that letters systematically represent sounds in spoken language is called the *alphabetic principle*. As they become print navigators, children learn that when letters are combined in a particular sequence, they represent individual words. They also learn that the sequence of letters is very important. For the word *top*, the sequence of letters is t-o-p; the word does not say *top* if we write p-o-t because the sounds that the letters represent are in a different order. (See Chapter 3 for more on sound–letter relationships.)

Print, like speech, is divided into words. Printed words do not change between readings of the same text. If we read and reread a favorite storybook, the words on the page and the words we say as we read aloud will always stay the same. In the early preschool years, children may begin to point along as they "read" familiar books or other texts. Show children that a word you are saying aloud is represented by one written word on the page by demonstrating how to point to each word as you read aloud. Children probably won't yet be able to point accurately, but they can develop their understanding of how print works by watching, listening, and applying what they're learning. Later, as children begin to try to decode words, they will know that a space on the page and a pause in speech signals when one word ends and another begins. This understanding enables children to attend to the beginning and end of a word and to learn that words have a first letter, a last letter, and a middle letter or letters. Understanding these print concepts is critical for figuring out the sounds those letters represent when decoding text. (This is discussed in more detail in Chapter 3.)

Print Concepts to Teach

Important print concepts for children to learn in early childhood include the following:

- Print carries meaning and represents language. It is what we read and write.
- Print is written by people called *authors.*
- Print can be used for many purposes, such as to inform, entertain, and persuade.
- Print can be found in many places, such as on some signs, on maps, and in books.
- Print follows a particular direction (called *directionality*).
- Books have a right side up and a front and a back.
- There is a right side up for print, and the orientation of letters matters.
- There's a place in a text where we start reading.
- Letters represent sounds (in English and other alphabetic languages).
- Letters make up words (in English and other alphabetic languages).
- Words don't usually change between readings.
- In print, we signal a new word by having a space with no markings. This understanding is called *concept of word.*
- Words have a beginning and an end.

Concepts of Pictures

In addition to learning about print, children learn concepts about how pictures work in text.

- **Concept of action.** Even though pictures are still, they can represent movement. For example, a picture of someone kicking a soccer ball represents the movement of the kicker and the ball.
- **Concept of intentionality.** Authors and/or illustrators choose or create pictures to accomplish a purpose, such as to make a reader laugh.
- **Concept of permanence.** Pictures in printed texts are permanent and do not change.
- **Concept of relevance.** Pictures and written text are related. If you've seen a young child draw a picture that doesn't go with the written words, you've seen a child who hasn't yet learned this concept.
- **Concept of representation.** Pictures represent objects, but they aren't the actual objects. For example, you can't actually drink a picture of a bottle of juice.
- **Concept of partiality.** Not everything in written text must be represented in the pictures. For example, two events might be described in a page of a story, but only one of them may be shown in the picture.
- **Concept of extension.** Some pictures provide information that is not in the printed words. For example, illustrations and graphics (such as diagrams) in informational texts for young children may show details that are not included in the text.
- **Concept of importance.** Some information in a picture may be more important than other information. You'll find that young children sometimes focus on a detail in a picture and need help to notice the picture's main idea.

Adapted, by permission, from N.K. Duke, R.R. Norman, K.L. Roberts, N.M. Martin, J.A. Knight, P.M. Morsink, & S.L. Calkins, "Beyond Concepts of Print: Development of Concepts of Graphics in Text, Pre-K to Grade 3," *Research in the Teaching of English* 48 (November 2013), 175–203.

Concepts of pictures are similar to concepts of print. Both are essential knowledge that help children navigate and understand books and other types of text.

Showing

Talking about the print in books is an important way to teach children about print. During read alouds, teachers can support learning by intentionally pointing to and discussing features of print with children. This technique is called *print referencing* (Justice & Sofka 2010).

Print Referencing During Read Alouds

Drawing children's attention to print is a powerful way to improve children's understanding that print conveys meaning. Print referencing also helps children learn about how print is organized and that print is made up of symbols (letters) that represent parts of language (words).

RESEARCH NOTE

The Impact of Print Referencing

Research with 4-year-olds shows that print referencing during read alouds can improve children's understandings about print in preschool and can have lasting effects on children's reading development (Justice et al. 2010; Piasta et al. 2012).

Many children's books are written and illustrated in ways that make the print particularly noticeable. These features make it easy to talk about the print with children. For example, the word *wiggle* might appear in a special font that makes it seem to wiggle across the page or text might appear in a speech bubble that shows what a character is saying (Zucker, Ward, & Justice 2009). Books with these kinds of features are called *print salient texts*. In these texts, the print and illustrations may be integrated in ways that enhance the text's message. These books are useful tools for print referencing because they make it easier for teachers to draw children's attention to concepts of print. Choosing print salient texts for read alouds is a teaching strategy that supports children's growth as print navigators.

Book	Print Salient Features
The Pigeon Wants a Puppy! by Mo Willems	Speech bubbles, visible sound (*aaaargh!*)
Growing Vegetable Soup, by Lois Ehlert	Environmental print in the illustrations (for example, labels of garden plants); text in bold or unique fonts
Chicka Chicka Boom Boom, by Bill Martin Jr. and John Archambault, illustrated by Lois Ehlert	Letters in isolation; changes in the print direction and color
Counting with Frida/Contando con Frida, by Patty Rodriguez and Ariana Stein, illustrated by Citlali Reyes	The same words written in English and Spanish; numbers written as numerals and as words
Little Blue Truck, by Alice Schertle, illustrated by Jill McElmurry	Visible sound (*oink, beep, bump*); changes in print direction and color
Secret Pizza Party, by Adam Rubin, illustrated by Daniel Salmieri	Environmental print in the illustrations (such as Uncle Mark's pizza sign)
Truck, by Donald Crews	Environmental print in the illustrations; text in bold or unique fonts
Jump! by Tatsuhide Matsuoka	The word *boing* depicted in different ways as specific animals jump; repetition of the word *jump*
Homemade Love, by bell hooks, illustrated by Shane W. Evans	Print of different sizes, print curved and linear; varied placement of print on the page

Table 2.1. Print Salient Texts

Approaches to Print Referencing

Teachers can engage children in conversations about print while reading aloud with the following techniques (Zucker et al. 2009):

1. **Pointing and tracking print.** Teachers point to specific words or track a finger under specific text while reading. Tracking is especially effective when there are a few words on a page.
2. **Making comments that reference print.** Teachers comment while reading aloud, such as "I start reading here" or "This is the letter *b*. I see three *b*'s on the page."
3. **Asking questions or making requests.** Teachers invite responses from children by asking questions, such as "Can you find the letter *k* on this page?," "Where do I start reading?," or "Can you spy the word *pizza* on this page?"

These approaches can be combined. For example, a teacher might combine pointing and asking ("Is this the letter *k*?" or "Do I start reading here or here?"). Teachers can also combine all three strategies into one interaction by asking, "Where do I start reading on the page?" After a child answers, the teacher can point and say, "Yes, I start reading here."

TEACHING TIP

Develop a Foundation for Reading

When print referencing, the goal is not yet to teach children to decode words. Rather, it is to develop a foundation for reading by helping children become familiar with print concepts. The goal is to help children discover that print is meaningful, that print is organized in specific ways, and that print is made of symbols that represent language (Justice & Sofka 2010).

Instructional Targets for Print Referencing During Read Alouds

When teachers read aloud to children, they can engage children in print using instructional targets that can be organized into four broader categories (Justice & Sofka 2010):

› **Print meaning**
  - Print carries meaning. Example: Point to text while you read.
  - Print is different from illustrations. Example: Point out text that is part of illustrations, such as speech bubbles.

- **Book and print organization**
  - Arrangement of print (in English, left to right, top to bottom). Example: Tell children, "When I read, I start here."
  - Book organization (title page, author, pages turn from left to right). Example: Narrate your actions, "Now it's time to turn the page."
- **Letters**
  - Letters have distinct shapes and names.
  - Letters have different forms.
  - Letters map to sounds.
- **Words**
  - Words are different from letters.
  - Words are different from each other.
  - Letters make up words.
  - Written words map to spoken words.

When to Reference Print

To help children make discoveries about print, teachers can regularly engage in print referencing during read alouds. But you don't have to do it every time you read. Also, you don't need to stop on every page to talk about print. We recommend that you stop every few pages during a read aloud. Focus on one preplanned print concept per reading (such as pointing out the letters that spell a particular, meaningful word). You may want to reread the same book three or four times focusing on different print concepts each time.

Listening to a read aloud should be a pleasurable experience for children. In addition to print referencing, make sure to still discuss the meaning of the book. It's important not to let the focus on print concepts limit children's overall understanding of the meaning of the text and their delight in stories and information books.

Print Referencing in the Environment

In addition to read alouds, teachers can draw children's attention to the authentic print in their environments. In a print-rich classroom, there may be printed signs, schedules, labels, and so on. Teachers can use impromptu moments to draw children's attention to both general and specific features of print. These exchanges may be short, as little as a few seconds long.

For example, during a dramatic play scenario involving a restaurant, a teacher might have the following conversation with children:

> **Teacher:** Let's figure out what this part of the menu says. (*Points to two consecutive words on the menu.*)
>
> **Child 1 and Child 2:** *T!*
>
> **Child 3:** *S!*
>
> **Child 2:** Tyrese!
>
> **Teacher:** There's the letter *t*, like *Tyrese*, and that word is /t/: /t/ *taco.*
>
> **Child 2 and Child 3:** Taco!
>
> **Teacher:** And there's the letter *s*. That word is *salad*: /ssss/ *salad.* Let's read it together. (*Tracks print from left to right.*)
>
> **Teacher and children:** *Taco salad.*
>
> **Teacher:** I want to order a taco salad, please!

In this short exchange, the teacher drew attention to how print in English is read from left to right on a page as well as the sounds represented by specific letters. By engaging children in the conversation, the teacher encouraged the children to pay attention to the print on the page, modeling using terms like *letter* and *word.*

Opportunities for print referencing can happen throughout the day. Be alert to opportunities to show children how print works, especially with texts that are personally meaningful to them.

KEY PRACTICES

Designing and Including

Designing as a key practice includes the intentional planning and preparation of the classroom, schedule, and materials to provide a rich variety of learning experiences. **Including** is a key practice essential to welcoming every child to the learning experience, ensuring equal access to learning, and fostering respectful and affirming relationships.

Designing

As you design experiences to support young children's development of print concepts, you can begin by thinking about ways to use print to connect children's home practices and community experiences with early childhood classrooms. One important strategy is encouraging children to look for print in their homes and bring in the objects with print that they find or photos or drawings of objects with print. Examples might include

- Groceries (e.g., a cereal box, the wrapper on a bottle)
- Mail (e.g., letters, advertisements)
- Household equipment (e.g., a TV remote, a coffee maker, a measuring spoon)
- Phones (e.g., adults read news and send texts and emails on phones)
- TV (e.g., print on the screen during the football game or when adults watch the news)
- Texts adults in the home have written (e.g., errands list, recipes)
- Other texts adults read (e.g., books, magazines, brochures, screens, directions)

Early childhood educators can encourage children and their families to look for print in their communities, outdoors, and in public places. You can also take children on a neighborhood walk to hunt for print. You might find

- Traffic signs
- Signs on stores
- Labels (for example, in the pharmacy you might notice that labels tell the names of different kinds of medicine and how much they cost)
- Maps at the subway or bus stop
- Billboards
- Logos on people's clothing
- Menus in restaurants

When teachers create opportunities for children to notice and discuss print they find in their homes and communities, this builds an understanding of how and why we use print. These practices demonstrate that print is important in the real world and not just for school.

Provide Authentic Print Materials

Make connections between the print children see outside of school and opportunities to use print in the early learning setting by including authentic print materials in the classroom, such as order forms, maps, and signs. Provide these materials in centers, and encourage children to engage with print across the day. As children play with these materials, you can help them to notice the print. For example, if children are pretending to make brownies with an empty box of brownie mix, you might say, "This box has directions for how to make the brownies right here on the back. Let's read them together so we can see what to do."

TECHNOLOGY TIP

Technology and Print Concepts

You may have seen a popular YouTube video called "A Magazine Is an iPad That Does Not Work" (www.youtube.com/watch?v=aXV-yaFmQNk). A 1-year-old tries to get a magazine to respond like an iPad by tapping, swiping, and so on. This video illustrates an important point: technologies are making print concepts more complex. For example, the concept that words don't change—a book says the same thing every time we open it—is generally true. But this isn't necessarily true for online texts, which may be revised at any time, as in a weather site. Educators need to be aware of the ways new technologies might influence young children's developing understandings of print. At the same time, you can support children as they learn about books and other types of printed text that are still important in an academic or school environment. Children need to learn about all of the types of print that they experience in their lives, including learning about how print works in new technologies.

Including

To support children's development as print navigators, teachers must ensure every child is included in the learning process. It is important to remember that print concepts are different across named languages. Here are some examples:

- While English is read from left to right, Arabic and Hebrew are read from right to left. The symbols used to represent sounds in Arabic and Hebrew alphabets also look different from the symbols *(a, b, c)* used in English.
- In some languages, words are not made up of letters. For example, in Chinese, words are made of one or more characters, which correspond to whole syllables and, usually, to a meaning that can be combined with the meaning of characters and markings.
- The alphabet letters in Spanish look similar to the letters in English, but the letters represent different sounds in each language. For example, *j* makes the sound at the beginning of the English word *jam* in English and the sound at the beginning of the English word *ham* in Spanish (written *jamón*).

The idea that print concepts differ across named languages means that children growing up in multilingual families may learn print concepts at home that are different from the print concepts learned at school. As such, it is important for teachers to recognize and support the diversity of children's efforts to use and represent language in print as opposed to assuming that children's communicative attempts—both orally and in writing—are wrong.

Affirming Children's Home Languages

Early childhood educators should learn about children's home language practices and their literacy experiences so that they can include the ideas about print that children engage in and bring from home in classroom learning and conversations. As NAEYC's "Developmentally Appropriate Practice" position statement notes, "Educators strive to make sure that each child hears and sees their home language, culture, and family experience reflected in the daily interactions, activities, and materials in the early learning setting" (NAEYC 2020, 17). Invite families to share books or documents in languages they use at home. Children are excited and interested to learn about the ways words are represented in print across the languages written and spoken by friends' families in their classrooms and also around the world.

KEY PRACTICES

Engaging and Explaining

Engaging children with print is a key practice that happens throughout the day during planned activities, daily routines, and play. Through the key teaching practice of **Explaining**, teachers provide important support for learning print concepts.

Engaging

Print is all around us. In our daily lives, we encounter all kinds of print—signs, menus, labels, forms, books, and articles, just to name a few. Young children are exposed to this print too, but they need educators' help to learn that this print has meaning. In the early learning setting, teachers can create print-rich environments in which children regularly interact with print.

Books, Books Everywhere!

Young children benefit from having access to many books throughout the day. Infants benefit from books they can touch and play with. Toddlers are beginning to understand that a book is something that can be read aloud; they will begin to ask an adult or older child to read books to them. Preschoolers become interested in different kinds of stories and texts. Variety is important. Make sure that children have access to books that are stories as well as books that are *informational*, conveying information about the world or teaching us how to do something. It is also important to make sure that children see themselves and their experiences reflected in the books in the classroom. If your space is limited, rotating books over time is a good way to ensure diversity. Rotating the books that you display is also a good idea, as children are drawn to books that are displayed.

Include books in which the text provides the words to favorite songs and rhymes. This helps children learn to associate written words in a book with the words to a familiar song. For example, a child who is already familiar with the song "He's Got the Whole World in His Hands," a traditional African American spiritual, may be able to sing along to Kadir Nelson's picture book *He's Got the Whole World in His Hands*. By drawing attention to the print associated with the words the child is singing, the teacher helps the child understand the relationship between spoken (or sung) words and the words in print.

Creating classroom books is another strategy for engaging children with print. Children are often motivated to engage with class books that they have created with their friends. For example, in a preschool classroom, a teacher might facilitate the authoring of a picture book about the sounds that children hear at bedtime. Given the prompt, "When I go to bed, I hear . . ." the teacher can ask the children to "document" what they hear when they go to bed. Voice-to-text technology can help children "write" the words for each page in the class book. The answers can be multilingual and multimodal. For example, one child might say they hear "dulces sueños, mi amor," another hears "sleep tight," and another child might hear "wen-wen-wen" (the sound of a New York City ambulance). The process of creating a book together helps children to see themselves as authors and to associate written text with their own oral language.

Print on Display

Displays in the classroom are a powerful way to invite children to engage with print. These displays can be presented on walls, bulletin boards, display panels, or on other surfaces. The text might include children's writing attempts, messages for the children, and children's names. Rotate or change these displays regularly and in ways that are meaningful to children. If everything is routinely labeled in the classroom (for example, *chair, table, bathroom*), children might become so accustomed to seeing the labels that they stop paying attention. On the other hand, labels can become more meaningful when children are involved in creating the pictures and words on them. Add labels to the classroom as needed and when they are actually used. For example, at cleanup time when a child is confused about where to put a toy, invite that child to help create a label for a bin so that all the children know where to put specific toys when they clean up.

Engage with Print During Play

Young children benefit from opportunities to engage with print during play. Making print materials available as children play is one way to encourage children to explore these possibilities. This might include making reading materials (magazines, books) and writing materials (paper, markers, pencils) readily available to children during all types of play.

It is also helpful to provide print materials that are specifically aligned to the play center or area. For example, place texts about different types of structures to build right where children typically build with blocks. Books with images of apartment buildings, bridges, houses, and arches as well as books about building construction can give children ideas about new structures to build and how to build them. Show children how these materials can be used. For example, you might say, "Let's look at these books about bridges to learn more about what they look like and how to make them. Maybe this will give you some ideas for how to make your bridge."

Which literacy items belong in which play center? Think about the literacy activities that children are likely to do in that center. For example, for the dramatic play area, think about what print materials would typically be in the setting that is the focus of the dramatic play theme. Here are some examples:

- **Restaurant:** menus, cookbooks, notepads for taking orders
- **Doctor's office:** eye chart with letters, sign-in for patients, books and posters about the human body (such as a book about bones), prescription pad, forms to complete
- **Store:** labels or stickers for creating price tags, items with writing on them (such as a cereal box), catalogs, papers for making receipts
- **Theater:** large pages for making signs about the show, small blank books to make playbills, printed out scripts
- **Travel:** maps, brochures from different locations, blank journals (to draw what you see)
- **Garden:** seed packets, plant catalogs, books with images of gardens, labels for plants
- **Museum:** signs, a map of the building and exhibits, placards for each item in the museum

Often businesses and other organizations in the community are willing to donate materials for your play areas. Many teachers store the materials by dramatic play theme so they are available for the next time. Teachers play an important role in facilitating play and showing children how the print materials can be used. Note the suggestion later in this chapter about how to observe children interacting with materials and see the knowledge of print concepts that they are developing.

Explaining

Young children may not pay attention to print because it is not yet meaningful to them. To learn more about how print works, adults need to illustrate, engage with, and explain these ideas to children. This can happen in early childhood settings whenever print is used across the day. Many toddlers will begin to notice print when you point it out. You can explain and show how print works when reading and writing (see the discussion of print referencing earlier in this chapter). Teachers can also explain how print works at other times of the day.

Explanations About Print

Here are some examples of the types of explanations that help young children to understand more about print concepts.

- **As children arrive in the morning:** "Good morning, Mia. Let's put your jacket in your cubby. Can you help me find your cubby? It's the one with your name on it. Let's look for the *M* at the beginning of your name. There it is! (*Points to the name, points to the* M.) There is the *M*. It spells the sound /mmm/ for *Mmmia*. Let's put your jacket in the cubby with your name so that we can find it easily when it's time to play outside."
- **To help with routines:** "That sign says *STOP.* Don't forget to hang the stop sign on the door when you are going to the bathroom. That lets others know to stop and wait until you are finished before they take a turn in the bathroom."

- **When infants and toddlers are playing with or looking at books:** "Let's turn the book so that you can read the story. Now if you turn the page like this (*Turns page.*), you can see the next page."
- **When using print in your own work:** "Thanks for reminding me about the puzzles. I'm going to write a note for myself to help me remember to put out the puzzles first thing tomorrow morning. I am writing the word *puzzles*. Can you help me to pin the note that says *puzzles* to the bulletin board so it is the first thing I see tomorrow morning?"
- **During play:** "I notice that your building is not finished yet. Would you like to write a message to let friends know that you do not want them to clean it up? Let's work together to make a sign."
- **During meals and snacks:** "We are having strawberry yogurt today. I can tell because the word *strawberry* is written right here on the package. It's good to read the package so we can tell exactly what is inside."
- **Whenever you write a message or scribe children's words:** "When I write a word, I leave a space on either side of the letters in the word. That's how we know it is just one word."

TRANSITIONS

Use Transitions to Teach Print Concepts

Print helps support transitioning in early childhood spaces.

Signing in. Younger children can show that they are present by finding their name and moving it to a "Here" column to show that they have arrived. Older children can sign in by writing their names. Signing in or checking in upon arrival replicates a common use of print in real-life settings.

Knowing where to get and return shared items. Using pictures and images to show where things are kept in the classroom can help children find what they need and help make clean up easier. Including a space on the shelf that says *markers*, coupled with an image, will help children to know where to put the tub of markers.

Making choices. Children can use print to sign up for activities or to make choices in the classroom. If there is room for four children at a time in the block area, children can move their name card to a board that lists that center. After the spots are filled, other children know that they need to make a different choice.

Taking turns. Charts or other types of print can help children know when it will be their turn. This might include a classroom responsibilities or opportunities chart, ways for tracking who gets to choose the song to sing or book to read, and also visual ways to track that each child gets a turn to share work and ideas.

The more you explain print concepts to young children, the more they will understand that print is important and useful in their own lives. These kinds of explanations will help children notice print, understand how it works, and begin to use it as part of their own lives.

KEY PRACTICES

Observing and Responding

Observing children is a key practice that informs our understanding of children's language learning—where they are now in their development and what they are ready to learn next. What we learn through observation will guide us in effectively **Responding** to children in ways that support learning.

Observing

Observing is one way to look for evidence of children's growth as print navigators. You can see how their understanding of print concepts develops in their use of print, their attempts at writing, and how they engage with print during play. As children engage in activities across the day, use anecdotal notes to document their literacy development. Anecdotal notes are a way for teachers to concisely record their observations of children's literacy development—their behaviors, skills, interests, performance, and more.

	Age	Milestones in Print Concepts
Infants	Birth–12 months	• Older infants look at images in texts when educators point. • Older infants may manipulate soft books and board books to turn pages. • Older infants may attempt to manipulate digital texts (tapping or swiping a tablet screen).
Toddlers	1–3 years	• Holds book/text and pretends to read. • Pretends to write (using scribbles or marks on the page). • Looks at images in text and describes/narrates. • Can find the front of the book, open it, and turn to the next page. • Notices environmental print (for example, points out a street sign during a walk). • Recognizes previously read texts by their cover and images. • Interested in print/images on digital devices (for example, pretends to text on an adult's phone or likes pressing keys on keyboard).

Table 2.2. Milestones in Print Concepts

	Age	Milestones in Print Concepts
Preschoolers	3–5 years	• Recognizes and names some letters and other symbols (numbers, common signs) in text. • Describes and discusses images in text. • Shows understanding that books always say the same thing on the same page (recites memorized texts, saying the correct words on the correct page or corrects adults if they misread a word that the child has memorized). • Can show the difference between a letter and a word. • Understands what a word looks like in text (can point to a word). • Attempts to read words. • Attempts to write words using letter-like symbols or real letters. • Writing attempts align with the type of text (for example, the child might ask to make a card that is folded or to staple multiple papers together to make a "book"). • Wants adults to write dictated words (asks adult to write "I am playing with Elliot" below a picture drawn by the child). • Writes with estimated spelling (such as writing *R*, *RN*, or *RAN* for *rain*). (Estimated spelling will be addressed in more detail in Chapter 3.)

Table 2.2. Milestones in Print Concepts (continued)

Responding

Young children regularly interact with print in environments that are filled with books, labels, signs, and other texts. After observing how children interact with print, teachers can respond to and help them take the next step in their understanding of how print works. These responsive interactions need not take long but, when finely tuned to children's needs, provide powerful supports for learning.

Remember that the goal at this phase of development is not for children to read or write conventionally or form letters precisely. In early childhood, children are building a strong foundation for later literacy learning that will lead to a lifelong love of reading and writing. As teachers, we can respond to children in ways that help them gain an understanding of how print works and become print navigators.

When you observe the child . . .	You may respond by . . .
Infants	
Looking at an illustration in a book.	Pointing to the illustration while talking about what that illustration shows.
Holding a board book.	Helping the infant to hold a book right side up.
Manipulating pages in a book.	Demonstrating while reading. "We turn the page like this."

Table 2.3. Observing and Responding

When you observe the child . . .	You may respond by . . .
Toddlers	
Finding the front of the book, opening it, and turning to the next page.	Expanding the child's print knowledge. "I start reading here on the page." (*Points.*)
Noticing environmental print (such as a stop sign).	Drawing attention to the word. "That sign says the word *STOP*. It tells drivers to stop and look around before they keep driving" or "This says the word *lunch* because this is where we put our lunch boxes."
Writing with scribbles or marks that are separate from a drawing.	Validating this important milestone of understanding that print is separate from pictures. "Tell me about your writing." (*Points to the marks.*)
Preschoolers	
Naming specific letters in a text.	Elaborating on what the child has said, for example: "Yes, that's an *m*. It stands for the first sound in this word: *mmmacaroni!*"
Writing with seemingly random letters.	Remembering that these letters are likely not random because they are usually familiar letters in the child's name that the child has seen repeated over and over. Many preschoolers are not yet connecting the letters they write with the sounds they are trying to say. Help the child to see that letters and sounds connect by displaying the child's or a friend's name and drawing attention to the beginning letter and sound in the name.
Writing with estimated spelling. For example, writing *B* for *bat*.	Validating this important understanding that spoken words and sounds can be written down. Help them to hear other sounds in words by stretching out the word and repeating sounds as needed (more about that in the next chapter). For example, you could say *baaaattttt*, with the focus on the final sound of the word, encouraging them to add a *T* to write *BT* for *bat*.

Table 2.3. Observing and Responding (continued)

Moving Forward

Learning how print works is one of the major accomplishments of early childhood. You foster children's understandings of how print works when you

› **Know** how print concepts are learned and recognize that these conventions may differ in certain ways. Also know that children can become proficient and can benefit from engaging with multiple sets of print conventions.

› **Show** children how print works by pointing out and explicitly explaining print concepts during read alouds and throughout the day.

- **Design** learning experiences that include authentic print materials in centers and a variety of books and texts.
- **Include** the conventions of the written language(s) children are exposed to in their home and child care or preschool setting.
- **Engage** and invite children and families to share and discuss print from their homes and communities, bringing print artifacts to the care setting or sharing photos of those artifacts.
- **Explain** and discuss print throughout the day, such as when on walks and other field trips with children (reading the *open* sign on a store and discussing the letter *o* or the letter *a* in *abierto*).
- **Observe** children's emerging understandings about how print works and support them in extending those understandings.
- **Respond** to children in ways that support their developing understanding of print concepts.

The birth-to-5 years are an ideal time for children to learn how print works. Young children can delight in interacting with a print salient book during a read aloud. Children can feel capable when they use print to identify their block structure or to convey their love for a family member. Learning how print works in the early years will also help formal reading and writing instruction in elementary school make much more sense to children. In doing so, early childhood educators are supporting children to become powerful print navigators.

References

Duke, N.K., R.R. Norman, K.L. Roberts, N.M. Martin, J.A. Knight, P.M. Morsink, & S.L. Calkins. 2013. "Beyond Concepts of Print: Development of Concepts of Graphics in Text, Pre-K to Grade 3." *Research in the Teaching of English* 48 (November): 175–203.

Justice, L.M., A.S. McGinty, S.B. Piasta, J.N. Kaderavek, & X. Fan. 2010. "Print-Focused Read-Alouds in Preschool Classrooms: Intervention Effectiveness and Moderators of Child Outcomes." *Language, Speech, and Hearing Services in Schools* 41: 504–20.

Justice, L.M., P.C. Pullen, & K. Pence. 2008. "Influence of Verbal and Nonverbal References to Print on Preschoolers' Visual Attention to Print During Storybook Reading." *Developmental Psychology* 44: 855–66.

Justice, L.M., & A.E. Sofka. 2010. *Engaging Children with Print: Building Early Literacy Skills Through Quality Read-Alouds.* New York: Guilford Press.

NAEYC. 2020. "Developmentally Appropriate Practice." Position statement. Washington, DC: NAEYC. www.naeyc.org/resources/position-statements/dap.

National Early Literacy Panel. 2008. *Developing Early Literacy: Report of the National Early Literacy Panel.* Washington, DC: National Center for Family Literacy.

Piasta, S.B., L.M. Justice, A.S. McGinty, & J.N. Kaderavek. 2012. "Increasing Young Children's Contact with Print During Shared Reading: Longitudinal Effects on Literacy Achievement." *Child Development* 83: 810–20.

Zucker, T.A., A.E. Ward, & L.M. Justice. 2009. "Print Referencing During Read-Alouds: A Technique for Increasing Emergent Readers' Print Knowledge." *The Reading Teacher* 63: 62–72.

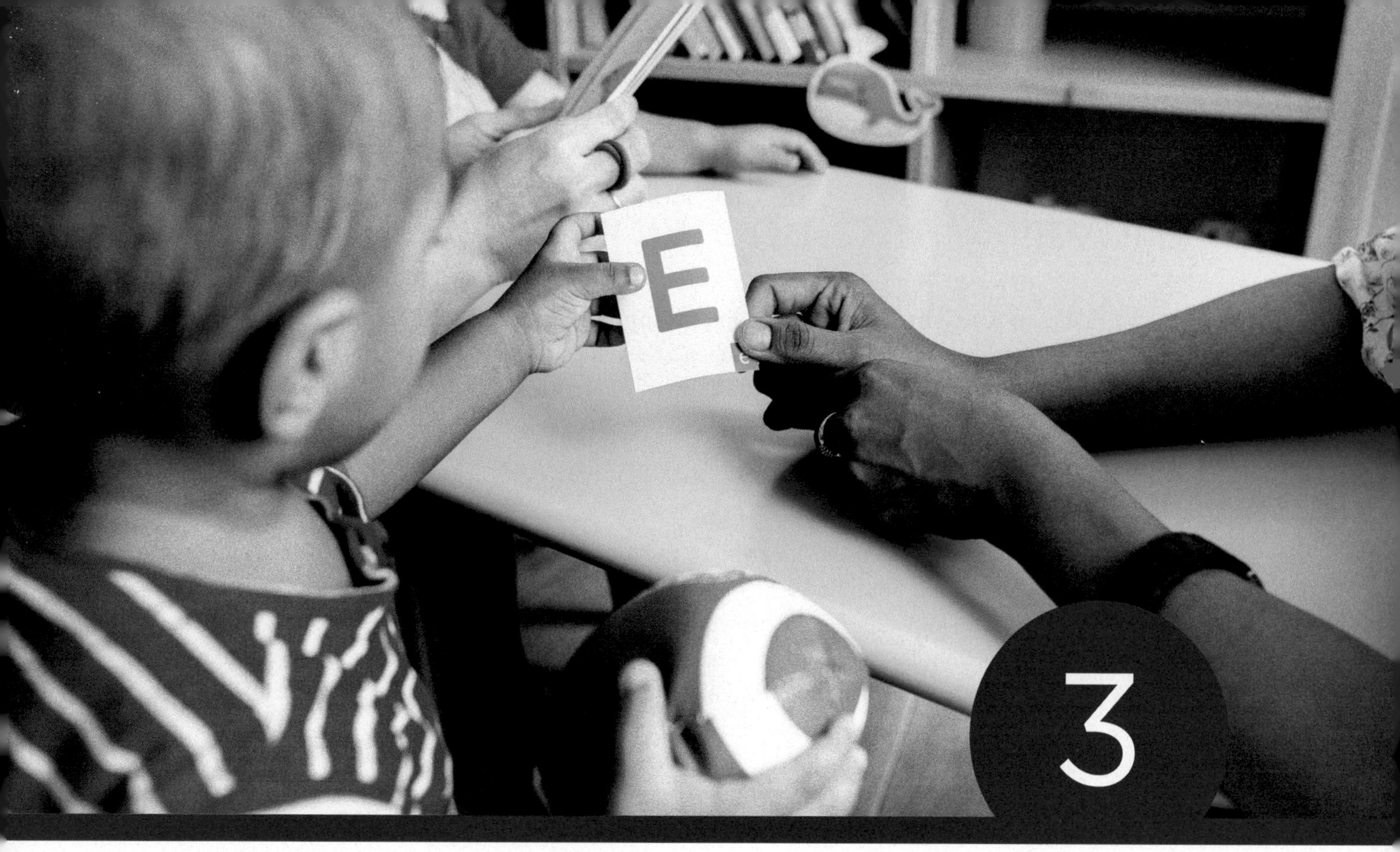

3

Sound-Letter Linkers

At bedtime, when my (coauthor Sonia Cabell's) son was about 3½ years old, we were talking about circles. Suddenly, his eyes widened, and he exclaimed, "I know! *S* is for *circle!*" I was thrilled because he was showing his understanding of the alphabetic principle. He perceived *circle* as a word independent from the shape. He could hear that it started with an /s/ sound, and he knew that *s* represents the /s/ sound (although in this word, it is spelled by the letter *c*, which can also represent the /s/ sound).

Young children love to play with the sounds in words. Many find it silly and entertaining, and all of this fun helps build the foundation for reading and writing. As children gain an understanding that oral language can be broken into smaller sounds (known as *phonological awareness*), they can apply this information by connecting individual sounds (*phonemes*) to the letters or groups of letters (*graphemes*) that represent these sounds.

In this chapter, we describe ways that teachers can support young children's development of phonological awareness and their understandings of the relationship between sounds and letters. These are exciting and important foundational understandings that move children toward conventional reading and writing. At the same time, these concepts are likely to vary across languages, and we explore this diversity as well.

KEY PRACTICES

Knowing and Showing

The key practice of **Knowing** is a starting point for supporting children's development of phonological awareness and alphabet knowledge as they become sound–letter linkers. **Showing**, another key practice, is an active response to Knowing.

Knowing

How do children learn to read words? It can seem to happen like magic, but there are predictable understandings that make it possible. As explained in Chapter 2, children learn the purposes of print and how it works—for example, the direction in which we read in a particular language and that letters (or other symbols) represent spoken sounds. As children become increasingly familiar with how print works, they may begin to recognize some personally meaningful words, such as their own name or the logo with the name of their favorite cereal.

The Learning Process

In an alphabetic language, such as English or Spanish, children need to learn to associate each individual letter and, eventually, groups of letters (such as *sh* or *ould*) with a sound or sounds. For example, children learn to associate the sound /d/ with the letter *d* and the letter *a* with the sounds at the beginning of *apple* and *acorn*.

Learning to blend sounds together to comprise a word is crucial for reading. For example, if the child sees *fan*, the child learns not only to say the sounds /f/, /a/, and /n/, but also to blend those sounds together to make /fan/. This is called *phonemic blending*. Once children go through this blending or decoding process a number of times, they come to recognize that word instantly. The amount of experience necessary to get to a point of recognizing a word instantly will depend on many variables—the length and complexity of each word, the child's interest and previous learning, and many other factors. But this experience in blending and decoding is important to achieving fluency in reading.

Understandings About Sounds

Children begin learning about the relationships between sounds and letters when adults and children engage in games and sing silly songs that play with spoken language. Through this kind of play in early childhood, children begin to understand that a word represents an object (for example, a cup is something to drink from) and has sounds in it (*cup* begins with the /k/ sound). As they continue to play with the sounds in words, children move toward *phonemic awareness*, which is the understanding that words are made up of individual sounds that can be combined to make words (Snow, Burns, & Griffin 1998). Phonemic awareness is essential to learning to read and write an alphabetic language, such as English or Spanish.

RESEARCH NOTE

Exposing Misconceptions About Learning to Read

You may have seen advertisements for products that claim to teach babies and toddlers to read or videos on social media showing a very young child's ability to "read." These ads and videos are compelling, but research suggests that these young children have probably memorized the words and are not actually decoding the words in printed text (Neuman et al. 2014). Many well-meaning teachers and families think that having children memorize words (through repetition or by using flash cards) will help them learn to read. While some children do get very good at memorizing a subset of words, research shows that memorization doesn't actually lead to reading well (Ehri 2017).

If children have only focused on memorizing words, when they encounter new words they haven't seen before, they typically do not know how to figure them out. And focusing on memorization may give children the false impression that memorization is how one learns to read. Children who are taught to memorize may be less likely to try decoding (figuring out how letters connect to sounds). Rather than asking children to memorize sight words and using flash cards, a more effective strategy is to work with children to support their understanding of the relationships between sounds and letters within and across languages spoken by the child.

Key Terms

- **Phonological awareness:** A broad term that refers to the awareness of the sound structure of an alphabetic spoken language, including the ability to manipulate it.
- **Phonemic awareness:** A subskill of phonological awareness that refers to the ability to identify and manipulate the smallest unit of sound that distinguishes one spoken word from another.
- **Phoneme:** An individual unit of sound that can distinguish one word from another (for example, /b/ and /m/ are different phonemes in English because /bat/ and /mat/ are different words).
- **Grapheme:** A symbol (in English and Spanish, for example, a letter or set of letters) that represent(s) a phoneme.
- **Alphabetic principle:** The understanding that alphabet letters represent spoken sounds in a systematic way.
- **Phonics:** An instructional practice that explicitly maps graphemes onto phonemes.
- **Spelling:** Connecting phonemes to graphemes to represent spoken words in print. From birth to age 5, the focus is estimated spelling, as explained in Chapter 4.

Phonological Awareness and Early Learning Standards

Of all the phonological awareness skills, the two most important in English are

- **Phonemic blending** (/f/, /a/, and /n/ can be blended together to say /fan/), which is necessary for reading
- **Phonemic segmentation** (the sounds in *map* are /m/, /a/, and /p/), which is necessary for spelling (and supports reading as well)

Educators do not expect preschoolers to fully master these skills, but it is important they begin developing an awareness of these processes and learning them in early childhood. Many state and national frameworks and standards include expectations that preschoolers will be able to engage in initial phoneme segmentation (identify the first sound in a spoken word, such as /b/ in the word *bus*) and that they will be able to orally blend an initial phoneme with the rest of the word (/b/ + /us/ = /bus/) (Administration for Children and Families 2015). These standards are created based on an understanding that, in English and other alphabetic languages, phonemic awareness in early childhood helps children connect the sounds of speech to letters so that they can learn to read and write (Ball & Blachman 1991).

How Children Develop Phonemic Awareness

Developing phonemic awareness, the subskill of phonological awareness that refers to the ability to identify and manipulate the smallest unit of sound in a spoken word, is not an easy feat. When we say a word, we don't really pronounce each separate sound. In fact, all of our speech runs together and we only stop to take a breath or at a pause. For example, say this sentence out loud: *Sheila went to the store and picked out vegetables.* Do you notice how all the words in the sentence run together and you are actually not pausing between each word when you talk? The only place you might pause is before the word *and*. It is not obvious to young children where one word ends and another begins.

Examples of Phonological Awareness

Examples of phonological awareness in English include

- **Rhyming.** *Dog* and *log* have the same sounds at the end.
- **Alliteration.** The words *big* and *boy* start with the same sound.
- **Sentence segmentation.** *I like pizza* has three separate words.
- **Syllabification**. *Dinosaur* has three syllables (each vowel sound in a word, with or without accompanying consonants, makes a syllable): di-no-saur.
- **Onset-rime blending and segmentation**. The onset /p/ can be blended with the rime /ath/ to make *path* (blending); the onset /p/ can be separated from the rime /at/ in the word *pat* (segmentation).
- **Phonemic awareness.** Attending to the smallest units of sound (phonemes) like identifying the phonemes /t/, /a/, and /n/ within the word *tan* or blending the sounds /f/, /i/, and /t/ to make the word *fit.*

When we think about individual words, we don't sound out each individual unit of sound (phoneme) when we talk. Take the word *pancake.* It's hard to figure out where one sound ends and another begins. The sounds in a word are analogous to the colors of a rainbow, a spectrum of light in which you can't really tell where one color ends and the next color begins.

Figure 3.1. The sounds in a word are analogous to the colors of a rainbow, a spectrum of light in which you can't really tell where one color ends and the next color begins.

TEACHING TIP

Start with Sounds That Are Easy to Stretch

Some phonemes in English make a sound that can be pronounced for several seconds without the sound changing, such as /f/, /l/, /m/, /n/, /r/, and /s/. These are called *continuous sounds*. As we teach children to blend and segment sounds, it may help to begin with words that start with these sounds so that children can more easily notice and isolate the first sound of the word.

Some phonemes in English make a *stop sound.* These sounds are pronounced briefly. Examples of stop sounds are /b/, /d/, /k/, /t/, and /p/. As you segment and blend words with these sounds, try to avoid adding /uh/ or another vowel sound to your pronunciation. It is not entirely unavoidable, but as much as possible, try to say /b/ rather than /buh/. This helps children to understand that stop sounds are single phonemes (represented by one letter) rather than two sounds /b/ and /uh/, which would need to be represented by at least two letters.

Phonemic awareness also involves developing the understanding that the sounds around a sound may affect that sound, especially in the case of vowels (Bear et al. 2020). For example, say these two words out loud: *pan, pat.* Notice how the /a/ sound is just slightly different between these words. That's because the /n/ in *pan* actually influences the pronunciation of *a*, as does the /t/ in *pat—a* is not always /a/. Breaking words into sounds can be challenging for children at first, which is why teachers should support children's phonemic awareness development during the early childhood years.

KEY IDEA

Foundational Concepts

As we support children's learning about sounds, it's important to remember these key ideas:

1. **Children generally become aware of larger units of language first, then move toward individual units.** Some children may not develop full phonemic awareness until kindergarten.
2. **Phonemic awareness is best learned along with letters.** It's not advisable to wait until children have developed phonemic awareness before working with letters. For example, sharing with children that the letter *c* spells the first sound in *color* can support phonemic awareness development and development of alphabet knowledge simultaneously, especially if we emphasize and repeat that initial sound and show the associated printed letter.
3. **Young children learn multiple phonological awareness skills at the same time.** Children don't have to master one skill before moving to another (Anthony et al. 2002; Phillips, Clancy-Menchetti, & Lonigan 2008). For example, children don't have to master rhyming before learning alliteration or beginning sounds in words. Development is not necessarily linear; this is especially the case for multilingual children. Attending to individual sounds (phonemic awareness) within named languages (such as English and Spanish) is the goal. It is helpful, therefore, to teach more advanced phonological awareness skills at the same time as less advanced skills.
4. **Don't focus only on rhyming.** Sometimes teachers think rhyming should be the main focus and expect it to be the easiest phonological awareness skill for young children (Phillips, Clancy-Menchetti, & Lonigan 2008). Research shows that some early childhood curriculum materials are also too focused on rhyming and not enough attention is given to other important phonological awareness skills (Skibbe et al. 2016). At least one study suggests that teachers may be able to skip rhyming and other phonological awareness skills entirely in preschool (Yeh 2003). Although we don't think there's enough research yet to recommend that, especially for infants and toddlers, we do recommend that you spend a lot of time on skills beyond rhyming. Phonemic blending (very important to decoding words) and phonemic segmentation (very important to spelling words) are the most important for children. Early learning standards do not require young children to get to a point where they can blend a lot of sounds in a word or segment every sound in a word, but according to the Head Start Outcomes Framework, by 60 months children should be able to blend at least two elements and segment at least the first sound in a word (Administration for Children and Families 2015).
5. **Sounds vary across alphabetic languages like English, Portuguese, and Spanish.** When teaching multilingual learners, remember that there are some phonemes in English that may not exist in other languages and vice versa. For example, the phoneme /th/ does not exist in Portuguese, and the grapheme ã and the phoneme /ẽ/ do not exist in English. Also, some graphemes are associated with different phonemes across languages. For example, *j* is associated with /j/ (in English), /h/ (in Spanish), and /ʒ/ (in Portuguese).

6. **Multilingual young children do not always sort their knowledge of language into what we label as *discrete/named languages.*** While acknowledging that languages are real, researchers have recently pointed out that they were created by adults (García & Kleyn 2016). This means that what we know as a language (English, Spanish, Mandarin, Japanese) is different from the language systems used by young children. Multilingual children draw from their entire language repertoires and are likely to experiment across what we label as different languages. These experimentations are not mistakes; they are part of young multilingual children's development. Understanding young children's communicative practices and contexts helps educators recognize that when multilingual children employ one language-specific phoneme to segment and blend phonemes in languages other than English, they are building phonemic awareness.

It's important to note that associations between letters and sounds are not universal; they are language specific (Souto-Manning & Martell 2016). In fact, the more expansive one's language repertoire, the more complex is the process of associating letters and sounds within the context of one language. As mentioned earlier, children do not naturally separate languages; this is a learned behavior.

One study focusing on alphabet knowledge in English found that being able to name 18 uppercase and 15 lowercase letters by the end of preschool is considered an optimal benchmark for successful reading later on (Piasta, Petscher, & Justice 2012).

RESEARCH NOTE

Alphabet Knowledge

At the same time as children are developing understandings about the sounds of spoken language, they also begin to develop understandings about how the alphabet works. Children do not need to master all phonological awareness skills before learning about letters. In fact, studies show that learning about sounds and letters together supports literacy learning (Ehri et al. 2001; Piasta & Wagner 2010).

In Chapter 2, we discussed the concepts of print that young children learn during early childhood. Young children also develop specific understandings about letters within print. In alphabetic languages, they learn about the shapes, names, and sounds of the letters of the alphabet. They learn that each letter of the English alphabet has an uppercase and a lowercase form. Many children recognize and write with uppercase letters before writing with lowercase letters.

As teachers support children's learning, it's important to know a few main ideas about how to teach alphabet knowledge:

1. **Teach lowercase and uppercase letters together.** For some letters, the uppercase and lowercase letter shapes are practically the same, just smaller or larger in size, as for *S/s* and *O/o*. For other letters, the shapes are somewhat different, as for *F/f* and *K/k*. For a few letters, the

shapes of their uppercase and lowercase forms are very different, as for *E/e* and *N/n*. Learning both lowercase and uppercase letters together will help children associate these different shapes with the same sound or sounds early on.

2. **Teach letter names and letter sounds together.** Children usually learn the names of letters before they learn their sounds. It is not known whether that is a natural tendency or whether it is because greater emphasis is often placed on letter names early on. Research that has been conducted in English suggests that educators should teach letter names and sounds at the same time. That is, educators should not first teach letter names and then later teach letter sounds.
3. **Teach children about the letters in their own names.** Children tend to learn the letters in their own name before other letters of the alphabet, especially the first letter of their first name (Justice et al. 2006). When you stop and think about your favorite letter, many people would say it is the first letter in their name; after all, it's a word they have heard, seen, and written a lot. Help children to learn how to write the letters in their names but also about the sound that each letter and/or group of letters represents.

TEACHING TIP

Letter Names and Sounds

Letter names can be confusing for young children for a number of reasons:

- **The same letter name can refer to different letters across languages.** For example, the name of the letter *e* in English is the name of the letter *i* in Portuguese.
- **The sound or sounds commonly associated with a letter may appear in different places in the letter's name.** For example, in English the sound commonly represented by the letter *v* is at the beginning of the letter's name: "vee." However, the sound commonly represented by the letter *s* is at the end of the letter's name: "ess."
- **Some letter names don't have a sound commonly associated with that letter anywhere in the letter's name.** For example, in English, the letter name for *h* does not have the /h/ sound (as in the beginning of the word *home*). The same is true for the letter names for *w* and *y.*
- **Some letter names that include a sound commonly associated with that letter don't necessarily include the sound we teach first to young children.** For example, the letter name for *c* has the /s/ sound, yet the /k/ sound for *c* is more common for words that start with the letter *c.*

As an early childhood educator, it's important to be aware of the complexity of letter names in English and in other alphabetic languages so that you can better understand and respond to what children may be doing and thinking. With all of these complexities, you might wonder whether you should even teach letter names. A research study compared teaching letter names and sounds to teaching letter sounds alone and found that teaching both letter names and sounds is most effective, at least in English (Piasta, Purpura, & Wagner 2010; see also Roberts 2021). We recommend teaching letter names and sounds simultaneously and placing equal or more emphasis on sounds.

The Alphabetic Principle

For children to break the code of reading and writing, they must integrate their knowledge of sound and print. A significant milestone is reached when children begin to understand that oral language is made up of smaller sounds and that letters represent those sounds in a systematic way. This is known as the *alphabetic principle.*

Once children have this essential understanding of the connections between sounds and letters, their knowledge of reading and writing will grow. Later, in kindergarten and first grade, with intentional and explicit instruction, children will begin to attend to all the letters in words. During this process, the brain makes connections between spoken and written language, enabling children to remember words "at sight" because they have repeatedly decoded the words, fully mapping phonemes with graphemes (Ehri 2017). As explained earlier, teaching sight words in preschool is not appropriate.

Showing

Early childhood teachers show children how to link sounds and letters by explicitly drawing children's attention to sounds and letters in words. As teachers point out these sound–letter relationships, children begin to pick up on these ideas and try them as well.

Strategies for Teaching and Showing

Point out words where the first sounds are the same. For example, you might say, "*Dog* and *door* both start with the /d/ sound."

Notice letters of the alphabet in the environment. For example, "I notice a sign that says *restroom*. That starts with the letter *r* which stands for the /r/ sound. Rrrrrr . . . estroom."

Compare the sounds and letters in children's names. For example, "*Joe, Jazlyn,* and *José* all start with the letter *J*, but the *J* in *José* stands for /h/ while the *J* in *Joe* and *Jazlyn* stands for the /j/ sound. Georgia's name also starts with the /j/ sound, just like *Joe* and *Jazlyn*, but in Georgia's name, the /j/ sound is spelled with the letter *G*."

Segment sounds and map letters to sounds when children watch you write. For example, "We are writing to invite families to visit our new art display outside our classroom. We want to say 'dear families.' Let's think, what is the first sound we hear in the word *dear*? /D/ . . . /d/ . . . /d/ . . . I hear a /d/ sound. So, let's write the letter *D* for the /d/ sound. Now let's think about the first sound we hear in the word *families* . . . /f/ . . . /f/ . . . /f/. What do you hear? What letter do we know that spells the /f/ sound?"

Help children learn to form letters. While preschoolers do not need to spend time trying to produce perfect handwriting on worksheets, it is important that children start to learn to make the shapes of letters. We want children to connect letter shapes, letter names, and letter sounds. Early childhood teachers should show children how to make letter shapes and then give them opportunities to make letters. Children don't need to be limited to traditional writing implements. Instead, they can make letters in sand, in foam, or with finger paint. Children can also draw letter shapes with their fingers in the air or make letter shapes with their bodies. Teachers can make giant letter shapes out of tape on the playground or the classroom floor and children can walk, jump, and hop on shapes of the letters. The goal is to help children begin to learn the shapes of letters and to connect these shapes to letter names and sounds.

TRANSITIONS

Teach Letters and Sounds During Transitions

Transitions are a great time to draw children's attention to the connections between sounds and letters. Many of the games and songs that children learn at other times can be repurposed to support transitions during the day. For example, you can invite children to transition (make a choice, go to a table, get packed up to go home) using strategies that emphasize sounds and letters in their names:

> If your name starts with the letter *T*, you can get ready to go outside.
>
> If your name starts with the sound /s/, it's time to wash your hands for lunch.
>
> If your name is /O/ /l/ /i/ /v/ /i/ /a/ (say each sound), it's time to choose your center.

You can also play games with other letters and sounds, during transitions:

> Let's figure out the word that I spy and then we can pack our bags. I spy something that starts with the /b/ sound.

Children also love to sing through transitions:

> Let's sing the alphabet song while we clean up today.
>
> Let's sing "Willoughby Wallaby Woo" about each friend's name before we go home today.

While transitions are not the time to teach new sound and letter activities, these provide wonderful opportunities to reinforce learning from other times of day.

KEY PRACTICES

Designing and Including

Designing as a key practice includes the intentional planning and preparation of the classroom, schedule, and materials to provide a rich variety of learning experiences. **Including** is essential to ensuring that every child sees themselves—their voices, values, practices—in the learning experience. Including is not simply about welcoming children; it is also about ensuring equitable access to and representation in learning, fostering respectful and affirming relationships, and working to foster true belonging.

Designing

Early childhood educators must design learning experiences that include and center children's experiences in their homes and communities in the early childhood setting. There are many ways to design opportunities for children to learn about sounds and letters, not only in lessons but also in the context of their families and communities. This is because children have already labeled (orally) places, persons, and things familiar to them. Building on this familiar knowledge offers a wealth of possibilities for learning.

Here we offer examples of how early childhood educators design and plan for experiences that bridge aspects of children's lives to foster their literacy development.

ABC Books

Think about ABC books. How might young children collect pictures of their preschool, homes, or neighborhood to create their own ABC books? ABC books can be multilingual and the words chosen to represent each letter can come from children's everyday lives. For example, in New York City, children who are 2, 3, and 4 years old may go to preschool by subway. Many of them help family members swipe the card that reads *MetroCard*. While *MetroCard* would be a hard word for young children in other contexts, it is familiar in the context of New York City. In fact, it is much more likely for children in New York City to have seen a MetroCard than a monkey, an animal often associated with the letter *m* and the sound /m/. Likewise, Mexican American communities may be familiar with tortillas and tamales but potentially not with turtles (as a word or an animal). (We discuss how to choose appropriate alphabet keywords later in this chapter.)

Food Labels

In a Head Start classroom, children were invited to bring in packages of food products they had at home (boxes, wrappers, and so on). The teacher then worked with the children to label the packages (cookies, Doritos, masa, Sazón), creating an ABC chart and an ABC book with items from children's

TECHNOLOGY TIP

Voice-to-Text Technology

In another preschool classroom, the teacher invited children to research what they heard when they went to sleep. She then invited the children to dictate what they heard into an iPad with a voice recognition (voice-to-text) function. The children were able to see their words represented by letters. The teacher also played the transcribed text out loud to the children so they could note any errors and approximations of their spoken words. Recognizing that approximations were part of the process of writing down words empowered children to try writing words themselves. This served as the beginning of a class text entitled "When I Go to Sleep."

homes. In doing so, the teacher also discussed how not every language is alphabetic. For example, a child brought a package of matzo crackers with writing in Hebrew and another child brought a bakery bag with writing in Chinese. Additionally, the teacher noted that while some alphabetic languages have the same letters, those letters can sound different. For example, comparing the name *Juan* to *juice* (from a juice pouch), the teacher was able to introduce this complex concept to children.

Games

Games like I spy are also favorites of young children. A toddler teacher may say, "I spy something that starts with /m/" to which a 2-year-old might respond, "My momma!" or "Maddie!"

KEY IDEA

Honor Family and Community Knowledge

In designing activities, it is important to build on what children already know, extend the knowledge their families and communities have, and affirm children's identities and language practices. This has been called *funds of knowledge* (Moll 2019) and *community cultural wealth* (Yosso 2005). Funds of knowledge and community cultural wealth are at the root of culturally sustaining teaching and learning regarding sounds and letters and any area of literacy development.

Funds of knowledge. The idea and practice of educators recognizing, documenting, and representing families' funds of knowledge, honoring the knowledge, resources, and strengths young children, their families, and communities possess, is central to quality early childhood education. It serves to challenge deficit orientations that are so dominant, in particular, in the education of children from families with low income, children of color, and immigrant children (Moll 2019). These deficit orientations lead educators to see children of color or from families with low or no income as being "at risk" or lacking "a proper upbringing," focusing on what children, their families, and communities lack, as opposed to focusing on what they do have—their practices, values, promise, and strengths. This is visible in how a teacher may see a multilingual child through a deficit lens, regarding them as lacking or having limited language.

Community cultural wealth. Community cultural wealth is an array of knowledge, skills, abilities, and contacts possessed and tapped into by communities of color to survive and resist oppression (Yosso 2005). This wealth can be aspirational (hopes and dreams), linguistic (intellectual and social skills gained through multilingual communication experiences and translanguaging practices), familial (rooted in community history, memory, and cultural intuition), social (networks of people and community resources), navigational (maneuvering through social institutions), and/or resistant (knowledge and skills cultivated by oppositional behaviors that challenge inequalities).

In one toddler classroom, two teachers collaborated to collect songs, rhymes, and chants children heard at home. Then, working alongside families, they wrote these chants down and produced audio versions of family members "reading" by singing, chanting, or rhyming. By associating written and oral language in meaningful ways, children in this class became more conscious of the connections between phonemes and graphemes across named languages and symbols. They then started making connections and expanding their knowledge, noticing and noting titles of published books, labels, and street signs starting with specific sounds.

Including

Belonging matters in the early years, and it is the responsibility of teachers to create classrooms where all children experience belonging. For this to happen, educators need to expand their expectations for what is considered typical and acceptable in their classrooms, preschools, and communities (Souto-Manning, Ghim, & Madu 2021). This is particularly important when the growing majority of young children is of color and multilingual (Cohn 2016; Frey 2019). Here are a few ideas for including young children's knowledge of sounds and symbols (including letters).

The Importance of Learning Pronunciations

People pronounce sounds differently. We all have different linguistic backgrounds and different accents. To communicate belonging, it is important that educators model an openness to learning how to pronounce names and words that are unfamiliar. To do so, teachers must engage in questioning which names and words are perceived as easy or difficult and which names and words sound familiar or unfamiliar. As much as educators may want to rely on their own perceptions, doing so can create spaces of exclusion. For example, when a teacher judges someone's name as "strange," "unfamiliar," or "extra," they are not likely to connect with that person on the same level as they do with someone whose name is familiar to them. In one example, an educator thought the name *Nevaeh* was strange and judged the family as a result, not understanding that the name *Nevaeh* is *heaven* spelled backward (Souto-Manning et al. 2018).

Creating inclusive spaces means helping each and every child to learn each other's names. A good resource for doing so is the book *Your Name Is a Song*, by Jamilah Thompkins-Bigelow, illustrated by Luisa Uribe. (The author also created a video pronouncing the names of all the book characters, which can be seen at www.youtube.com/watch?v=ZmXqJGherE8.) Singing songs with names representing multiple identities and linguistic backgrounds is another way to teach pronunciations. The importance of learning and pronouncing names can be shown through picture books, such as *Alma and How She Got Her Name*, by Juana Martinez-Neal, and poems like "My Name Is Jorge" in *My Name Is Jorge: On Both Sides of the River*, by Jane Medina, illustrated by Fabricio Vanden Broeck.

Reading about names and learning how to pronounce names are pathways for creating a more inclusive classroom. Additional pathways include making name books and exploring the different sounds made by the same symbol. Did you know that *Rita* is pronounced Rita (ree-tah) in English, Heeta in Portuguese, and Rhida ਰੀਟਾ in Punjabi? This is because *r* in the beginning of a word in Portuguese is pronounced with an /h/ sound and the letter *t* in the middle of a word in Punjabi stands for /d/. Regardless of these different associations between the same symbol and distinct sounds, teachers can work with children's own names as a springboard for learning about sound–letter relationships. When a child's name does not use English letter sounds or English sound–letter combinations, you can use such opportunities to make everyone aware of multilingualism. Teachers who are committed to fostering belonging talk about variation as an inherent part of language; after all, there is one truth about languages: they vary more than they remain the same.

There is no way educators will be familiar with every way of pronouncing a symbol. Because of this, it is important to take the time to learn instead of hurrying to correct sounds children may be associating with written symbols. Although a quick reaction, these corrections can communicate to children that there is something wrong with them or with the ways they communicate. For example, suppose a teacher asks children for the sound at the beginning of the word *snake* in English. Snake is *cobra* in Portuguese and *culebra* in Spanish. If a child makes the sound /k/ instead of /s/, that child is communicating their multilingualism and not their lack of knowledge. Here, instead of correcting the child, educators should seek to understand and learn from the child. Assuming that every child is operating from a linguistic stance similar to your own can be detrimental to learning. Instead, centering the belief that children are capable and full of valuable language practices and knowledge allows you to affirm—and not correct—children's accents, dialects, and language practices.

As mentioned earlier in this chapter, children do not automatically sort letters, symbols, and words into named languages (English, Portuguese, Spanish). This concept of discrete languages is something new that they will need time and support to learn. Multilingual learning takes time, and educators can patiently affirm children's developmental attempts to draw on their full and rich linguistic repertoires.

Teaching Accessible Sounds

Teachers can support the needs of children who are Deaf and hard of hearing by seeking advice from audiologists or teachers specializing in educating children who are Deaf. It may be important to learn which sounds should be taught earlier and to better understand how to help children learn letters and sounds. Multimodal shortcuts, such as using motions or pictures of items, can be especially important to helping children who are Deaf and hard of hearing to remember these sounds. Remember that different children will have different levels of hearing loss and may have a different range of sounds that are accessible. If a child is not repeating a sound, it may be because they cannot hear it. Again, do not hesitate to seek support from experts who can help you meet the needs of children who are Deaf or hard of hearing or any child in your classroom.

KEY PRACTICES

Engaging and Explaining

Engaging children in learning about letters and sounds is a key practice that happens throughout the day during planned activities, daily routines, and play. Through the key teaching practice of **Explaining**, teachers provide support for making sound–letter connections.

Engaging

Engaging with books and materials in the classroom plays an important role in developing young children's phonological awareness and their sound–letter knowledge (as does Explaining, discussed later in this chapter). Provide books and materials that encourage children to play with the sounds in languages in ways that highlight critical phonological awareness skills. Alphabet books and other materials help children learn to name letters and to connect letters with words that start with that letter.

Books

While planning read alouds to support children's phonological awareness and alphabet knowledge, we recommend choosing books that feature a range of opportunities to play with sounds.

RECOMMENDED RESOURCES

Sound–Letter Read Alouds

Rhyming books. With infants and toddlers, plan time for children to engage with rhyming books. As children become more familiar with these books, pause while reading to let them fill in the rhyming words. For example, you might say, "Brown Bear, Brown Bear, what do you see? I see a red bird looking at . . ." and then wait for the child(ren) to say *me*.

- *Giraffes Can't Dance*, by Giles Andreae, illustrated by Guy Parker-Rees
- *Goodnight, Goodnight, Construction Site*, by Sherri Duskey Rinker, illustrated by Tom Lichtenheld
- *Hush! A Thai Lullaby*, by Minfong Ho, illustrated by Holly Meade
- *Moo, Baa, La La La!* by Sandra Boynton
- *One Love*, by Bob Marley, adapted by Cedella Marley, illustrated by Vanessa Brantley-Newton
- *Twenty Big Trucks in the Middle of the Street*, by Mark Lee, illustrated by Kurt Cyrus
- *What Is Light?* by Markette Sheppard, illustrated by Cathy Ann Johnson
- *Whose Toes Are Those?* and *Whose Knees Are These?* by Jabari Asim, illustrated by LeUyen Pham

Alliteration books. While reading books with preschoolers that include alliteration (the same sound at the beginning of multiple words), stop to notice all of the words that start with the same sound. Invite children to think about other words they know that start with that sound.

- *B Is for Baby*, by Atinuke, illustrated by Angela Brooksbank
- *Bee-Bim Bop!* by Linda Sue Park, illustrated by Ho Baek Lee (rhyming and alliteration)

- *Clara Caterpillar*, by Pamela Duncan Edwards, illustrated by Henry Cole
- *Diez deditos/Ten Little Fingers and Other Play Rhymes and Action Songs from Latin America*, by José-Luis Orozco, illustrated by Elisa Kleven
- *Jamberry*, by Bruce Degan (rhyming and alliteration)
- *Mamá Goose*, by Alma Flor Ada and F. Isabel Campoy, illustrated by Maribel Suárez (rhyming and alliteration)
- *Many Marvelous Monsters*, by Ed Heck
- *Sleep Well Siba and Saba*, by Nansubuga Nagadya Isdahl, illustrated by Sandra van Doorn
- *Some Smug Slug*, by Pamela Duncan Edwards, illustrated by Henry Cole

Books that play with the sounds in words. As you read books that play with phonemes, invite children to play with these sounds. For example, in *Cock-a-Doodle-Moo*, by Bernard Most, the cow says "sock-a-noodle moo" and "rock-a-poodle moo." Invite children to make up other silly versions of rooster sounds that they invent (such as "lock-a-boodle-moo" or "rock-a-soodle-moo").

- *Cock-a-Doodle-Moo*, by Bernard Most (changing the beginning sound in words)
- *Don't Be Silly, Mrs. Millie!* by Judy Cox, illustrated by Joe Mathieu
- *Runny Babbit*, by Shel Silverstein (book of poems, swaps the onset of two different words)

Alphabet books. As explained elsewhere in this chapter, in preschool it's important to provide some alphabet instruction outside the context of books. However, alphabet books can complement that instruction, and they can be read to toddlers as well. As you read alphabet books with children, point out the letter name, the letter shape, a common sound or sounds associated with the letter, and images of words that start with that common letter sound. Invite children to add their own words that start with the sound that is the focus on that page. For example, on a page focused on *m*, you can say, "We see a *mouse* and the *moon* and some *milk*. What other words do you know that start with *m* and make the *mmmm* sound?"

- *A Is for Activist*, by Innosanto Nagara
- *A Is for All the Things You Are: A Joyful ABC Book*, by Anna Forgerson Hindley, illustrated by Keturah A. Bobo
- *A Is for Awesome! 23 Iconic Women Who Changed the World*, by Eva Chen, illustrated by Derek Desierto
- *Chicka Chicka Boom Boom*, by Bill Martin Jr. and John Archambault, illustrated by Lois Ehlert (focus on letter recognition)
- *Eating the Alphabet: Fruits and Vegetables from A to Z*, by Lois Ehlert
- *Just In Case: A Trickster Tale and Spanish Alphabet Book*, by Yuyi Morales

With nearly any alphabet book, you will find that not every word represents the sound or sounds you want to teach for that letter. For example, noting that "*a* is for *all*" may be appropriate for the substance of a specific alphabet book, but the word *all* does not include either of the sounds for the letter *a* that we recommend teaching in preschool (which are *a* as in *apron* and *a* as in *animal*). When this situation occurs in an alphabet book, focus on the name and shape of the letter but not the sound. Save your comments about the sound(s) associated with the letter for pages with good keywords for that letter. For more about quality alphabet keywords, see later in this chapter.

KEY IDEA

How to Introduce Vowels

In English, vowels represent many sounds, but we don't need to teach children all the sounds at once. Most vowels represent a range of different sounds in English words depending on the spelling of the word. Let's consider the letter *a*, which can stand for

- The short /a/ sound in *apple*
- The long /a/ sound in *acorn*
- The schwa sound (that is, the vowel sound in an unstressed syllable) in *agree*

A also changes to a different sound when it is combined with other letters (for example, in the words *aardvark* and *airplane*).

When reading books with toddlers and preschoolers, it is fine to read all of the keywords that are associated with a letter, but doing so can also be a bit confusing for children. It is okay to start by focusing on words that start with the long and the short vowel sounds. In most variations of English, *a* stands for the long /a/ sound at the beginning of *acorn, angel*, and *ape* and the short /a/ sound at the beginning of *astronaut, apple*, and *alligator.* However, there are also dialectical variations in pronunciation that are important to acknowledge; for example, the words *pecan* and *aunt* may be pronounced differently depending on the dialectal variation. As children learn more about letters and sounds, they will have time to develop their understanding of all of the sounds that individual vowel letters and combinations of vowel letters can represent.

Songs and Movement

Recently, I (coauthor Tanya Wright) was on a video call with my 4-year-old nephew. When we were greeting each other, he said, "Hi, Aunt Tanya, Fanya, Banya, Manya, Lanya" and burst out laughing as if this was the funniest thing he had ever heard. I responded with, "Hi, Reuben, Meuben, Teuben, Feuben. I think I know a song that you are going to really like." Then I taught him "The Name Game," by Shirley Ellis. This led to much more laughter as we sang the song over and over again, changing the first sounds in the names of everyone in our family.

Just like in this example, teachers can promote children's learning about sounds and letters through songs, rhymes, and movement. The goal for these activities is to have fun. Children should be encouraged to participate as much as possible through singing, chanting, movement, and even making up their own versions of songs.

› **Fingerplay and movement songs**
  - "Five Little Ducks" (rhyming and counting)
  - "Itsy Bitsy Spider" (rhyming)
  - "One, Two, Buckle My Shoe" (rhyming and counting)
  - "Teddy Bear, Teddy Bear, Turn Around"

› **Songs where children make up their own rhymes**
  - "Down by the Bay"

› **Songs that play with first sounds in children's names**
  - "The Name Game" (Felix, Felix, bo-belix, Banana-fana fo-elix, Fee-fi-mo-melix, Felix!)
  - "Willoughby Wallaby Woo" (Willoughby Wallaby Wanya, an elephant sat on Tanya)

› **Alphabet songs**
  - "The Alphabet Song" (we recommend a more staccato version, such as the version from the television show *Super Why!*)
  - "Who Let the Letters Out?"

Children also love to play with the beginning sound(s) of words. Start by taking a familiar song that children know well and change the first sound(s) in each word of the lyrics. So, for example, sing "Row, Row, Row Your Boat," but start each word with the /b/ sound. For words that start with one sound, such as *row*, change the first sound only (*row* becomes *bow*). For words that start with a consonant blend (like the *dr* in *dream* or the *str* in *stream*), remove the blend and replace with the new sound (*stream* could become *beam*):

Bow, bow, bow bour boat
Bently bown ba beam
Berrily, berrily, berrily, berrily
Bife bis but ba beam.

Have fun, and get silly! Pick a new first sound to try each time you sing it.

Materials for Learning About Sounds and Letters

Include a range of materials in the classroom to promote children's learning about sounds and letters. It is helpful to show children how to use these materials and then make them available to children during self-directed play.

Alphabet charts and alphabet strips. Display an alphabet chart (each uppercase and lowercase letter with a keyword or keywords pictured) in the classroom for children's reference. Make sure that children can easily see the alphabet chart (not too high on the wall) and that you reference it regularly so they learn how to use it. For example, children might use the chart if they are trying to write a word and need to figure out which letter to use to represent a sound. Having small versions of the alphabet chart in other places, such as a writing center, can also be very helpful to children.

Materials for sound–letter sorts. These are baggies or bins of pictures or objects that represent words that start with different sounds. You might include pictures of objects with names that start with the /s/ sound and others that start with the /m/ sound. Children can then sort these pictures into different piles to represent different sounds. For example, children might put the pictures of the sun, socks, a sink, and a sandwich in one pile labeled with the letter *s* for words that start with /s/ and they might put pictures of the moon, milk, a mouse, and a mouth in a different pile labeled with the letter *m* because these words start with /m/. This is a great activity for preschoolers to work on with their peers. Encourage children to discuss why they sorted a picture into a particular pile.

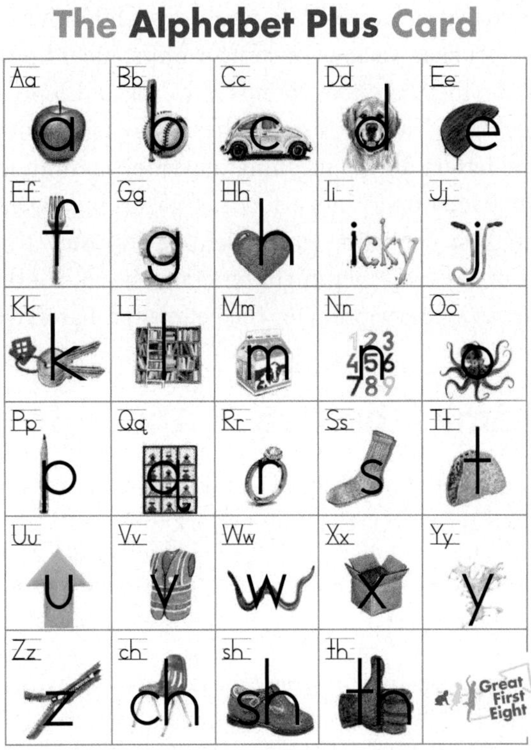

Figure 3.2. An alphabet chart can be used to promote children's learning about sounds and letters. It is helpful to show children how to use these materials and then make them available to children during self-directed play.

Reprinted with permission. The Great First Eight Curriculum (GreatFirstEight.org), 2022, Regents of the University of Michigan.

TEACHING TIP

Tips for Sound–Letter Sorts

When you work with preschoolers on picture sorts based on sound–letter relationships, make sure they can identify the picture in oral language before starting the sort. Sometimes children may not know the word for a particular picture or may know a different word for that picture. For example, a child might look at a picture that is intended to be a mouth for the /m/ sound and say "lips." This can cause confusion about how to sort the words by their first sound. Ask children to name the pictures and, if they use a different word, validate the children's responses and then share the word for the picture in this particular sort.

Writing materials. To encourage children to write as part of their play, incorporate writing materials in various learning centers, including the writing and dramatic play centers. As children write, they listen for sounds in words and represent these words with letters (known as *estimated spelling*). This work is a fantastic way for children to practice what they have learned about sounds and letters during meaningful written communication (see more on this in Chapter 4). To transform this kind of play into a successful learning experience, it is critical for the teacher to interact with children, modeling and explaining how they are using the writing tools in meaningful ways. For example, a teacher might first take the role of the veterinarian who fills out a medical chart and writes a prescription for the pet owner. Later, children can take over this role.

Games that Teach About Sounds and Letters

There are many types of games that support young children in learning about sounds and letters. The suggestions that follow work well for toddlers and preschoolers in small group settings.

Picture sorts. Children sort pictures into groups by the first sound in the words represented by the picture (see "Tips for Sound–Letter Sorts").

I spy. Take turns spying objects that start with a particular sound and the rest of the group guesses what it is: "I spy something that starts with /d/." You can also play this game with letter names: "I spy something that starts with a *d*."

Robot talk. Say words by segmenting their sounds using a funny robot voice. Children can guess which word you are saying: "This is my /p/ /e/ /n/." The sillier teachers get with this game (really trying to make a robot voice or moving your body like a robot), the more fun this will be for children.

Say it, move it. As children figure out a sound in a word, they move a token for that sound. For example, for the word *cat*, children would push one token for each sound: /c/, /a/, and /t/. Children can then "trade" the tokens for letters. For letter sounds children already know, start with the letters rather than tokens.

Tracking games. Having young children use their fingers to track the alphabet letters on a chart while singing the alphabet song can help them to learn their letters. You can start by singing the first few letters slowly. Watch as a small group of children track along with you on their individual charts (or alphabet arcs). Help them to accurately track with a few letters and gradually add more.

Matching games. Using an alphabet chart, children can match magnetic or tile letters to the corresponding letter on the chart. There are many ways to create matching letter games. For example, during the fall, teachers might create construction paper leaves to make a simple puzzle. Put an uppercase letter on top and its corresponding lowercase form on the bottom and cut in a zigzag between them. Matching letters to children's names is a great way to start!

Other games. There are so many other games that could help children learn the alphabet. Here is a brief list:

- Alphabet bingo
- Lotería

Wondering About Worksheets and Flash Cards?

Sometimes early childhood educators may avoid teaching children about sounds and letters because they connect this work with inappropriate practices for young children, such as worksheets and flash cards. We agree that children should not spend time on worksheets and flash cards in early childhood classrooms! However, as we've seen in this section, there are brief lessons and a lot of enjoyable learning opportunities that are engaging for young children. Young children can and should learn about sounds and letters in ways that are playful, fun, and developmentally appropriate. Just like in the example with Tanya's nephew, if we choose appropriate methods, supporting young children's learning about letters and sounds will feel joyful and exciting.

- Puzzles in which children assemble the alphabet or where children match a letter to an image with the correct beginning sound
- Guessing the letter in a mystery bag based on its shape by feeling it and giving a clue about the word's sound(s) (for example, what sound it starts with or what sounds it rhymes with)
- Using children's names and friends' names to learn letters
- Going on a letter hunt in the classroom
- Filling a bag with items that begin with the same sound as the letter written on the bag (also a great at-home activity to engage families with children's learning)

Whatever the game, it is important to guide children and make sure they are understanding and practicing the task accurately to reinforce their learning of alphabet knowledge.

Explaining

If we had to select just two words to describe how to explain phonological awareness and alphabet instruction, those words would be *brief* and *clear*. Here are some examples of brief and clear instruction for young children:

- "Rhyming words have the same sounds at the end. *Ball* and *tall* rhyme. *Ball* and *tall* both have the *-all* sound at the end." (phonological awareness)
- "When you say *fox*, the first sound you say is /f/. Fffffox." (phonemic awareness)
- "Your name starts with the letter *L*. *L* stands for the /l/ sound. That's the sound at the beginning of your name: Lllatrese!" (alphabet instruction/phonics)
- "The letter *o* is a circle shape. The letter *o* stands for the /o/ [oh] sound or the /o/ [ah] sound." (alphabet instruction/phonics)

Notice that these statements are brief and clear.

RESEARCH NOTE

Developmentally Appropriate Practice

In the field of early childhood education, there is the misconception that it is developmentally inappropriate to be explicit in instruction with young children. However, there is no research to support that position. NAEYC's "Developmentally Appropriate Practice" position statement states that "when planning learning environments and activities, educators may find it helpful to consider a continuum ranging from children's self-directed play to direct instruction. Neither end of the continuum is effective by itself in creating a high-quality early childhood program" (NAEYC 2020, 9). Learning about sounds and letters is a time when we believe it is developmentally appropriate to be direct or explicit with young children—we cannot expect young children to figure all of this out on their own or we are likely to advantage children who are receiving such instruction within their homes and communities, upholding inequities (Delpit 1988). Again, the key is to be brief and clear.

Important Instructional Ideas for Cultivating and Sustaining Sound–Letter Linkers

- For infants, we do not recommend providing alphabet instruction. To date, there is little reason from research to think that such instruction will be helpful to children this age.
- For toddlers, we recommend providing explanations about letters and sounds only when questions or opportunities arise. For example, if a child is trying to write their name or is making a stop sign for their construction project, that's a great time to be explicit.
- For preschoolers, we suggest not only being explicit when questions and opportunities arise, but also providing systematic and explicit alphabet instruction. *Systematic instruction* means having a system or plan to ensure that over time you teach and review the name and the major sound or sounds associated with each alphabet letter in meaningful and developmentally appropriate ways. Research shows that both 3- and 4-year-old children can develop alphabet knowledge when provided with systematic instruction in 10- to 15-minute lessons, with no negative impacts on their motivation (Roberts 2021).

Systematic Alphabet Instruction

What is systematic alphabet instruction? And in what order and at what pace should you teach the alphabet? It is tempting to think that you should start with *a* and go to *z* and teach one letter per week, but research suggests that both this order and pacing do not make the most sense (see, for example, the book *No More Teaching a Letter a Week* [McKay & Teale 2015]). Instead, make sure you are teaching and reviewing multiple letters each week and be purposeful. Research has not revealed one ideal order of alphabet instruction, but here are some suggestions:

- Teach more letters earlier in your sequence of instruction that are continuous or stretchable sounds.
- Teach letters earlier on that occur more frequently in English (such as *r* and *s* before *q* and *v*).
- Teach at least one vowel (we recommend the letter *a*) early on so you can start to model blending consonant-vowel-consonant words (such as *sat* and *lap*), further reinforcing what letters and sounds can be used for.
- Wait until later in the year to teach letters that do not have a target sound of the letter in the letter name (such as *h*, *w*, and *y*).
- Avoid teaching letters together if the letters are easily confused visually (they look similar, such as *o* and *q*) or auditorily (they sound similar, such as *i* and *e*).

Some letters will be easier to learn; for example, children tend to learn the letters in their own names earlier than other letters. Some letters are harder to learn than others, requiring more review and uneven amounts of review for different children. In preschool, tracking which alphabet letters each child knows by name and by sound(s) can help to guide you in planning which to review with which child(ren).

RESEARCH NOTE

The Value of Decontextualized Alphabet Teaching

Among early childhood educators there is a misconception that children should not be taught alphabet letters out of context. Put another way, many believe that the alphabet should only be taught in the context of books. However, research suggests that stand-alone lessons about letters and sounds are actually more effective. This is not to suggest that you shouldn't talk about letters in the context of books as well (see the Chapter 2 discussion of print referencing during read alouds, for example), but rather that it is important to also take time to focus specifically on letters and sounds (Roberts, Vadasy, & Sanders 2020).

An approach to teaching about sound–letter relationships that seems to be especially helpful for children is *paired associate learning*. In this approach, children are taught to associate a letter with a keyword that begins with a sound commonly associated with that letter, such as an object (*a* is for *apple*) or character (*b* is for *big bear*). This approach is especially helpful if children can see the letter embedded within a picture of that object or character (Ehri, Deffner, & Wilce 1984).

In addition to the one keyword, educators can share other words that begin with the major sound(s) of that letter as well, including words that are important to individual children (for example, their names) and to children's communities (such as names of valued places in the community). Begin with one keyword or phrase that children especially associate with the letter.

Figure 3.3. The paired associate learning approach supports alphabet learning. It can be especially helpful to embed lowercase letters in a picture of an object whose name begins with that letter and target sound.

Choosing appropriate alphabet keywords. A quality alphabet keyword (or phrase) should begin with a sound commonly associated with the letter, such as *bat* for the letter *b* or *dog* for the letter *d*. One keyword is needed for each consonant. Possible exceptions where two keywords may be needed are the letter *g* (one for the hard /g/ sound, as in *goat*, and one for the soft /g/ sound, as in *giraffe*) and the letter *c* (one for the hard /c/ sound, as in *cat*, and one for the soft /c/ sound, as in *celery*). We say "possible" because the research is not yet clear about the benefits of teaching two sounds for these letters in the preschool years. What is clear is that two words should be taught for each vowel, one for the vowel's long sound, which is also its letter name, and one for the vowel's short sound (as in *apple, edge, iguana, octopus*, and *umbrella*).

An exception to this pattern is the letter *x*. Many people teach *x* is for *xylophone*, but that is such an uncommon sound–letter association for *x* that we recommend instead teaching a word with *x* at the end, as in *box*. Notably, /x/ actually represents two sounds at the same time (/ks/). In English, /q/ also almost always represents two sounds (/kw/).

TEACHING TIP

Selecting Keywords

1. **Make sure that the keyword really does begin with the target sound.** For example, *orange* is not a good keyword for the letter *o* because it neither begins with the long /o/ sound nor the short /o/ sound. (Rather, it begins with what's called an *r-controlled vowel sound.*)
2. **Make sure that the keyword does not begin with a different letter's name.** For example, *cake* is not a good keyword for the letter *c* because it begins with the name of the letter *k*. *Elephant* is not a good keyword for the letter *e* because it begins with the name of the letter *l*. That can be quite confusing for children.
3. **The keyword should not begin with a blend** (two or more consonant letters/sounds pronounced in succession in a syllable; the /fl/ in *flat*, the /cr/ in *crab*, and the /tw/ in *twinkle* are all consonant blends), especially if the first sound in the blend is a stop rather than continuous sound. This is because it can be particularly difficult for children to segment only the first sound within a blend.

For example, *drum* does not work well as a keyword for the letter *d* in part because it is hard for children to segment the /d/ sound in /dr/. That said, depending on children's phonemic awareness development, the time of year, and other factors, you could try such a word as an alphabet keyword.

4. **The keyword should be familiar to or easily learned by children.** Such words may vary depending on the children's backgrounds and may not match what is familiar to you (see the "Including" section earlier in this chapter for further discussion).
5. **The keyword should be something that can be depicted easily.** For example, *apple* works well for many children because it is easily recognized in a drawing or photograph.
6. **The keyword should not be something that is easily confused with another item that begins with a different sound.** For example, /b/ is for *boat* can be problematic because children may be inclined to say "ship."
7. **The keyword should not be something that would be a problem for certain religious or other cultural groups.** For example, *jack-o-lantern* is not a good keyword for *j* because it is associated with a holiday that not all families observe.
8. **Some names make good keywords and others do not.** Children's names are a powerful tool for literacy learning, but not all children's names make good keywords. For example, the name *Juan* is not, in English, a good keyword for the letter *j* because it does not represent a sound commonly associated with *j*. Similarly, *Aubrey* is not a good keyword for the letter *a* in English because the name does not begin with the short or long sound of *a;* knowledge of *au* for the "aw" sound is not expected in the preschool years. However, you can value each of these names (and any words that are not good alphabet keywords) by simply explaining; for example, "Juan's name starts with the /h/ sound—that's another sound the letter *j* can make." Names and words that do not make for good alphabet keywords can also help children learn what the letter *looks* like; for example, "Aubrey's name helps us see the shape of *A*. See the slanted line up and then back down with a line across?"

Finally, as you choose alphabet keywords, consider the ways in which children in your classroom speak. The alphabet keyword should begin with a sound that matches how children pronounce the sound associated with that letter, not how you do. You may even need to choose multiple keywords to account for all of the pronunciations represented in the classroom.

KEY PRACTICES

Observing and Responding

Observing children is a key practice that informs our understanding of children's language learning—where they are now in their development and what they are ready to learn next. What we learn through observation will guide us in effectively **Responding** to children in ways that support learning.

Observing

Observing is one way to look for evidence of children's developing understandings about sounds and letters. As you observe children's development, it is important to remember that multilingual children may recognize and use sounds and symbols from multiple languages.

Milestones in Learning About Sounds and Letters

The table that follows lists developmental milestones for children who have experienced continuity in language across contexts. These do not apply to children who did not grow up speaking English or in an English-speaking familial or community context. Note that children as young as 2 years old can start developing phonological awareness, but most development tends to happen from ages 3 to 6. Some of these developmental tasks are easier to learn and others are harder. Harder tasks may take longer for children to learn. For example, it is easier to recognize rhymes than to produce rhyming words. For phonemic awareness, it is easier to blend sounds to form a word (for example, the teacher says /c/ /a/ /t/ and the child says "cat") than to segment them (child says the /c/, /a/, and /t/ sounds in *cat*).

	Age	Literacy Development: Milestones in Learning About Sounds and Letters
Infants	By approximately 12 months	• Attends when adults produce sounds; for example, when they sing songs and recite rhymes. • Coos and babbles. *(Note that while these examples for infants do not represent phonological awareness, these are behaviors that can support phonological awareness development later.)*
Toddlers	By approximately 3 years	• Participates in rhyming songs and chants. • Fills in missing rhyming words in familiar songs and chants. • Attempts to clap along with the beat during songs and rhymes. • Produces some letter-like forms and scribbles. • Makes marks, symbols, or drawings to represent ideas. • Begins attending to letters in their name. • Shows increasing interest in print in books and print in their environment.
Preschoolers	By approximately 5 years	• Participates in games and songs that play with sounds in words. • Recognizes the same initial sounds in different words (for example, *mat* and *mouth* start with the same sound). • Orally blends two sounds when an adult provides phonemes (for example, adult says "/g/ /o/" and child says "go").

Table 3.1. Milestones in Learning About Sounds and Letters

	Age	Literacy Development: Milestones in Learning About Sounds and Letters
Preschoolers (continued)	By approximately 5 years (continued)	• Identifies first sounds in words in oral language (for example, when asked what is the sound at the beginning of the word *dog*, child says "/d/"). • Recognizes and names at least half to two-thirds of uppercase and lowercase letters of the alphabet (if growing up speaking the language of instruction). • Provides sounds and keywords for some letters of the alphabet. • Forms letter shapes for some letters of the alphabet. • Writes own name. • Attempts to write some words using estimated spelling (for example, may represent first sound in words, such as *D* for *dog*, or represents some sounds in words, such as writing *MT* for *empty*).

Table 3.1. Milestones in Learning About Sounds and Letters (continued)

Responding

After observing how children interact with sounds and letters, teachers can respond to help them take the next step in their understanding of how sounds and letters work. The more you know about children's understandings, the better you are able to build on what children know to support next steps. Educators figure out what children understand about sound–letter relationships by listening to what they say and also by watching what they do. Listen to children as they participate in the activities described in this chapter but also look carefully at their early writing attempts for clues about what children know: observing children informs teachers' formal and symbolic curriculum and teaching (Gay 2002; Souto-Manning et al. 2019).

When you observe the child . . .	You may respond by . . .
Infants	
Attending during songs, rhymes, and fingerplays.	Encouraging children to participate by inviting them to join in on words or to clap along.
Toddlers	
Chanting along with a familiar rhyme.	Inviting the child to fill in the missing rhyming word.
Beginning to recognize their own name.	Pointing out the sounds that each letter represents. ("The *S* in your names stands for the /s/ sound in *Sebastian.*")
Noticing text in the environment.	Naming individual letters that represent sounds in the child's name. ("The *m* in that word stands for the /m/ in *metro.*")

Table 3.2. Observing and Responding

When you observe the child . . .	You may respond by . . .
Preschoolers	
Figuring out the first sound in a word.	Inviting the child to think of other words that start with the same sound. Inviting the child to listen for other sounds in the word.
Attempting to write letters.	Showing the child how to form the letter and connect this with the sound of the letter and a keyword. ("This is how you make the letter *f*. Remember that *f* makes the /f/ sound like in the word *fish*.") Inviting the child to try making the letter.
Orally blending sounds (you say /h/ /a/ /t/ and the child can say *hat*).	Encouraging the child to try segmenting sounds. ("What is the first sound you hear in the word *hat*? What is the next sound that you hear?") Helping them to hear the sounds in words by stretching out the word (*"haaaattttt"*).
Orally identifies the first sound in words (if you ask, what is the first sound in the word *paint*, the child responds with "/p/").	Inviting the child to write words using estimated spelling. Helping children to represent the sounds they hear with letters. For *paint*, a child may just write a *P* or they may write *PT* or *PAT*. All of these spelling attempts demonstrate that the child is working on representing sounds with letters—this should be encouraged.

Table 3.2. Observing and Responding (continued)

Moving Forward

Supporting children's phonological awareness and alphabet knowledge development is one of the important contributions you make as an early childhood educator. Among other things, you foster children's phonological awareness and alphabet knowledge when you

- **Know** how children develop phonological awareness and alphabet knowledge, including technical matters, such as why phonemic blending and segmentation are so important to literacy and how letter names can cause confusion.
- **Show** children the connections between letters and sounds by providing materials that support alphabet development, such as alphabet charts and materials for word sorts.
- **Design** opportunities for children to learn about sounds and letters in the context of their families and communities, such as by bringing in examples of print in their communities and discussing the sound–letter relationships represented.
- **Include** children by considering their languages and ways of pronouncing sounds, rather than your own, when interacting with children around the alphabet, choosing alphabet keywords, and so on.

- **Engage** children by singing songs that involve playing with sounds, reading books that involve play with sounds and/or that reinforce specific alphabet knowledge, and playing games that involve sounds and letters, such as I spy (for example, "I spy something that starts with the sound /m/").
- **Explain** concepts to children by being explicit about letter names, sounds, and shapes when questions or opportunities arise and provide, for preschoolers, brief (10–15 minute), systematic, and explicit lessons about letter names, sounds, and shapes.
- **Observe** children's emerging understandings of phonological awareness and alphabet knowledge and support them in extending those understandings.
- **Respond** to young children's literacy practices, supporting, expanding, and extending their development.

There is a lot to consider in this chapter. Some ideas may seem familiar and others may seem very new. Take your time. You may find that it takes practice, patience, and multiple readings of the chapter to incorporate these strategies into your classroom. Your continued attention to this important area of development is essential for sound–letter linkers.

References

Administration for Children and Families. 2015. *Head Start Early Learning Outcomes Framework: Ages Birth to Five.* Washington, DC: US Department of Health and Human Services. https://eclkc.ohs.acf.hhs.gov/sites/default/files/pdf/elof-ohs-framework.pdf.

Anthony, J.L., C.J. Lonigan, S.R. Burgess, K. Driscoll, B.M. Phillips, & B.G. Cantor. 2002. "Structure of Preschool Phonological Sensitivity: Overlapping Sensitivity to Rhyme, Words, Syllables, and Phonemes." *Journal of Experimental Psychology* 82 (1): 65–92.

Ball, E.W., & B.A. Blachman. 1991. "Does Phoneme Awareness Training in Kindergarten Make a Difference in Early Word Recognition and Developmental Spelling?" *Reading Research Quarterly* 26: 49–66.

Bear, D.R., M. Invernizzi, S. Templeton, & F.R. Johnston. 2020. *Words Their Way: Word Study for Phonics, Vocabulary and Spelling Instruction.* 7th ed. Hoboken, NJ: Pearson.

Cohn, D. 2016. "It's Official: Minority Babies Are the Majority Among the Nation's Infants, But Only Just." *Pew Research Center*, June 23. www.pewresearch.org/fact-tank/2016/06/23/its-official-minority-babies-are-the-majority-among-the-nations-infants-but-only-just.

Delpit, L. 1988. "The Silenced Dialogue: Power and Pedagogy in Educating Other People's Children." *Harvard Educational Review* 58: 280–98.

Ehri, L.C. 2017. "Orthographic Mapping and Literacy Development Revisited." In *Theories of Reading Development*, eds. K. Cain, D.L. Compton, & R.K. Parrila, 127–46. Amsterdam: John Benjamins.

Ehri, L.C., N.D. Deffner, & L.S. Wilce. 1984. "Pictorial Mnemonics for Phonics." *Journal of Educational Psychology* 76 (5): 880–93.

Ehri, L.C., S.R. Nunes, D.M. Willows, B.V. Schuster, & Z. Yaghoub-Zadeh. 2001. "Phonemic Awareness Instruction Helps Children Learn to Read: Evidence from the National Reading Panel's Meta-Analysis." *Reading Research Quarterly* 36: 250–87.

Frey, W.H. 2019. "Less Than Half of U.S. Children Under 15 Are White, Census Shows." *Brookings*, June 24. www.brookings.edu/research/less-than-half-of-us-children-under-15-are-white-census-shows.

García, O., & T. Kleyn, eds. 2016. *Translanguaging with Multilingual Students: Learning from Classroom Moments.* New York: Routledge.

Gay, G. 2002. "Preparing for Culturally Responsive Teaching." *Journal of Teacher Education* 53 (2): 106–16.

Justice, L.M., K. Pence, R.B. Bowles, & A. Wiggins. 2006. "An Investigation of Four Hypotheses Concerning the Order by Which 4-Year-Old Children Learn the Alphabet Letters." *Early Childhood Research Quarterly* 21 (3): 374–89.

McKay, R., & W.H. Teale. 2015. *No More Teaching a Letter a Week*. Portsmouth, NH: Heinemann.

Moll, L.C. 2019. "Elaborating Funds of Knowledge: Community-Oriented Practices in International Contexts." *Literacy Research: Theory, Method, and Practice* 68 (1): 130–38.

NAEYC. 2020. "Developmentally Appropriate Practice." Position statement. Washington, DC: NAEYC. www.naeyc.org /resources/position-statements/dap.

Neuman, S.B., T. Kaefer, A. Pinkham, & G. Strouse. 2014. "Can Babies Learn to Read? A Randomized Trial of Baby Media." *Journal of Educational Psychology* 106 (3): 815.

Phillips, B.M., J. Clancy-Menchetti, & C.J. Lonigan. 2008. "Successful Phonological Awareness Instruction with Preschool Children: Lessons from the Classroom." *Topics in Early Childhood Special Education* 28: 3–17.

Piasta, S.B., Y. Petscher, & L.M. Justice. 2012. "How Many Letters Should Preschoolers in Public Programs Know? The Diagnostic Efficiency of Various Preschool Letter-Naming Benchmarks for Predicting First-Grade Literacy Achievement." *Journal of Educational Psychology* 104 (4): 945–58.

Piasta, S.B., D.J. Purpura, & R.K. Wagner. 2010. "Fostering Alphabet Knowledge Development: A Comparison of Two Instructional Approaches." *Reading and Writing* 23: 607–26.

Piasta, S.B., & R.K. Wagner. 2010. "Developing Early Literacy Skills: A Meta-Analysis of Alphabet Learning and Instruction." *Reading Research Quarterly* 45: 8–38.

Roberts, T.A. 2021. "Learning Letters: Evidence and Questions from a 'Science of Reading' Perspective." *Reading Research Quarterly* 56 (1): 171–92.

Roberts, T.A., P.F. Vadasy, & E.A. Sanders. 2020. "Preschool Instruction in Letter Names and Sounds: Does Contextualized or Decontextualized Instruction Matter?" *Reading Research Quarterly* 55: 573–600.

Skibbe, L.E., H.K. Gerde, T.S. Wright, & C.R. Samples-Steele. 2016. "A Content Analysis of Phonological Awareness and Phonics in Commonly Used Head Start Curricula." *Early Childhood Education Journal* 44: 225–33.

Snow, C.E., S.M. Burns, & P. Griffin, eds. 1998. *Preventing Reading Difficulties in Young Children*. Washington, DC: National Academies Press.

Souto-Manning, M., B. Falk, D. López, L. Barros Cruz, N. Bradt, N. Cardwell, N. McGowan, A. Perez, A. Rabadi-Raol, & E. Rollins. 2019. "A Transdisciplinary Approach to Equitable Teaching in Early Childhood Education." *Review of Research in Education* 43 (1): 249–76.

Souto-Manning, M., H. Ghim, & N. Madu. 2021. "Toward Early Literacy as a Site of Belonging." *The Reading Teacher* 74: 483–92.

Souto-Manning, M., C. Llerena, J. Martell, A. Maguire, & A. Arce-Boardman. 2018. *No More Culturally Irrelevant Teaching*. Portsmouth, NH: Heinemann.

Souto-Manning, M., & J. Martell. 2016. *Reading, Writing, and Talk: Inclusive Teaching Strategies for Diverse Learners, K–2*. New York: Teachers College Press.

Yeh, S.S. 2003. "An Evaluation of Two Approaches for Teaching Phonemic Awareness to Children in Head Start." *Early Childhood Research Quarterly* 18: 513–29.

Yosso, T.J. 2005. "Whose Culture Has Capital? A Critical Race Theory Discussion of Community Cultural Wealth." *Race, Ethnicity, and Education* 8: 69–91.

4

Resourceful Writers

I (coauthor Mariana Souto-Manning) read the book *Colorful Leaves*, by Maria Fleming, to my 4-year-old son. After we intentionally attended to the labels of different leaves, I noticed that he started drawing and labeling pictures of leaves. He wrote *PAN* to label the picture of a pine leaf.

I decided to take him for a walk around the neighborhood to collect leaves. As we walked, we talked about leaves. Upon our return, my son used *Colorful Leaves* as a resource and engaged in labeling the leaves he had found.

Figure 4.1. In this image, a child is labeling leaves and writes *PAN* for *pine*.

Figure 4.2 shows his labeling of *wait oak* (white oak); he wrote *wait* for *white* and mixed lowercase and uppercase letters.

He also created a label for a leaf he did not recognize, inspired by one of his favorite animals (the three-toed sloth, from an episode of *Go, Diego, Go!*). He made a label for the leaf, shown in Figure 4.3 as *three tud leaf*. He initially wrote *tree*, then corrected his labeling after referencing

Figure 4.2. This leaf is labeled *wait oak* for *white oak.*

Figure 4.3. A child writes *three tud leaf*, building on knowledge about three-toed sloths.

Figure 4.4. A child writes *barc* for *bark.*

environmental print (a box with the word *three* printed on it). *Toed* was initially written as *tod* and then changed to *tud*. With encouragement from me, he wrote the word *leaf* with a mirrored *f*.

I knew that discussing print within the context of the environment around my 4-year-old son would likely lead to important lessons about writing. As this brief example illustrates, he used estimated spelling to label the leaves, drawing upon his own knowledge of how writing works.

Later, while walking with his dad, he employed collecting and labeling skills, expanding his repertoire from leaves to other tree parts, such as *barc* (for bark), seen in Figure 4.4.

When young children are immersed in an environment where adults discuss the print around them and where adults model writing tasks, they become interested in making their mark. At first, infants and toddlers may play and scribble with writing materials, such as markers and chalk. In preschool, children begin to represent their ideas using pictures, symbols, and alphabet letters. Young children are resourceful writers, using what they know about how print works; about the relationship between sounds and letters; and about their worlds to share their stories, knowledge, and ideas.

In this chapter, we discuss major areas of writing development—composing, spelling, and handwriting—and describe how teachers can intentionally support children's sharing of ideas through writing.

KEY PRACTICES

Knowing and Showing

The key practice of **Knowing** is a starting point for supporting children's development of early writing skills. **Showing**, another key practice, is the active response to Knowing.

Knowing

Engaging in writing is an important part of young children's literacy learning experience. Indeed, research shows that teaching writing can actually foster reading development (Graham & Hebert 2010, 2011). It may feel like young children aren't really writing because their marks don't look like conventional letters until around the age of 4. And even then, their spellings are estimates of words based on their knowledge of sounds and letters. But there's more to early writing than meets the eye.

KEY IDEA

Three Major Areas of Writing

Writing includes many types of knowledge and skills (Graham 2018). Three of the major areas (Berninger 2009; Kaderavek, Cabell, & Justice 2009) include

- Composing
- Spelling
- Handwriting

When children write, they engage in all three areas simultaneously. For example, when writing a note to a friend, a child generates a message (composing) using physical marks (handwriting) to approximate or produce words (spelling).

Composing

Young children have important things to say—stories, information, ideas, and opinions to share! When adults model for children that their ideas can be written down, children begin to understand that their own stories can be captured in written language. *Composing* is the act of generating and organizing ideas for writing (Berninger & Swanson 1994).

Why is it important to support children's early composing development? One reason is that composing is linked to oral language learning, supporting children's vocabulary and syntactic knowledge development (Kim & Schatschneider 2016). In addition, composing can lead young children to see connections between spoken and written language. They see that what they say can be written down.

Children's early composing often starts out as telling what they know (Bereiter & Scardamalia 1987). Adults might be doing the writing as young children dictate their thoughts, and it may be very simple at first. An adult may write down exactly what a child says: *Rashida said, "I winned the game!"* During dictation, adults should not correct children's language but rather write down children's words exactly as spoken. This helps children understand that their own words can be represented in print.

Figure 4.5. Images with letter-like figures mixed into the drawing.

Figure 4.6. Young children compose by drawing and telling about their drawing.

In addition to dictation, children might be doing the writing on their own. Often, writing starts with drawing. At first, it may be difficult to decipher the messages children are writing without asking them for clarification. For example, in Figure 4.5, a child's mother wrote down the child's dictated words: *I baked brownies with Nana*. Notice that the drawing looked more like brownies than like letters of the alphabet, although there are letter-like figures mixed into the drawing.

Young children are very capable of sharing longer messages and stories. In Figure 4.6, a young child explains their drawing and the dictated words are written by the adult.

Over time, the oral narratives that young children tell (both fiction and nonfiction) increase in length and become better organized (Stadler & Ward 2005). This reflects children's oral language development. Adults can write down these narratives as children dictate words and sentences.

It is also important to note that when children come back to the same drawing or writing later on, they may provide an explanation or description that is different from what they first reported. This happens even when children are writing with letters and demonstrates that they haven't yet grasped the alphabetic principle (Owocki & Goodman 2002), an understanding of the relationships between spoken sounds and written letters (see Chapter 3).

Learning to compose is not linear. Even though children's oral language will develop over time and their ideas and narratives become more sophisticated, young children's composing will develop and change as they understand new ideas about how the alphabetic system works in English. As they begin to understand that what they write corresponds to the sounds of language, children may write less on a page, rather than more. For example, young children's compositions may demonstrate brief estimated spellings (such as writing *LFT* for the word *elephant*). Their once longer texts may become very short because of their growing awareness that letters make up words and those letters are mapped onto the sounds of spoken language.

Spelling

How young children spell words showcases their early understanding of how written language works. It might sound strange to use the word *spelling* to describe young children's written marks (such as *LFT* for *elephant*, as noted earlier) because the words are not at all conventionally spelled. But long before conventional spelling takes place, young children learn many print concepts (see Chapter 2) and they display their knowledge, to some degree, in their writing. For example, as seen in Figure 4.7, a child might write by scribbling from left to right on a page, showing that they understand that we write from left to right in English.

During early childhood, a child's writing may become more recognizable to an adult reader. For example, see how this child writes *Happy Birthday* in Figure 4.8.

Clearly, there is a lot of development that takes place in the early years. Research shows that young children's spelling relates to their later writing and reading ability (National Early Literacy Panel 2008). But this spelling development doesn't just unfold naturally—it is fostered when teachers provide scaffolded support to children (Cabell, Tortorelli, & Gerde 2013; Ouellette, Sénéchal, & Haley 2013).

Figure 4.7. Writing through scribbling from left to right.

Let's consider how spelling develops over the early years. We will discuss four important phases of spelling (Cabell, Tortorelli, & Gerde 2013):

1. Drawing and scribbling
2. Letter-like forms and random letter strings
3. Salient and beginning sounds
4. Beginning and ending sounds

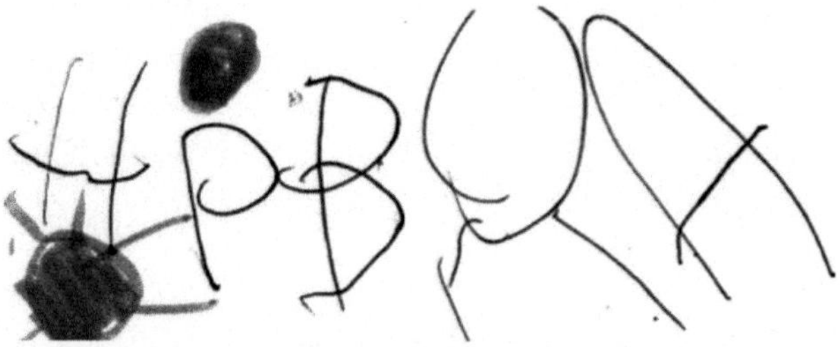

Figure 4.8. A child writes *happy birthday* using letters to represent many sounds in the words.

Drawing and scribbling. At first, young children often don't make a distinction between drawing and writing. When you ask them to write something, they might draw instead. Their drawing *is* their writing. Then, children begin to develop an awareness that writing consists of marks that are separate from their drawings. For example, they might draw a picture of themselves and write their name next to it as a small squiggle, as seen in Figure 4.9.

Figure 4.9. A child draws squiggles to represent writing.

Young children love to experiment with writing. Toddlers will play with writing tools, like markers, crayons, and chalk. Toddlers often make circular scribble marks. These early marks are not necessarily considered "writing" because the child is not intending to communicate a message through the marks. They are simply playing with the tools they see adults use around them to accomplish tasks. Over time, they realize that marks can carry meaning.

As children grow and learn, their scribbles begin to carry meaning. For example, a young child may use directionless scribbles to stand for familiar words (e.g., *daddy, mommy*). Over time, children's scribbles reflect the directionality of the language (left to right, top to bottom on a page in English) and start to look like writing.

TEACHING TIP

Celebrate Scribbling

Some teachers and children view the word *scribbling* as negative. But children's writing of all kinds should be celebrated! This is why we don't say that children are "just scribbling." While recognizing that scribbling is an important phase of development, we are not suggesting that teachers should talk to children about which phase they are in. Rather, we are sharing a framework for teachers to better understand development so they can support young children's efforts.

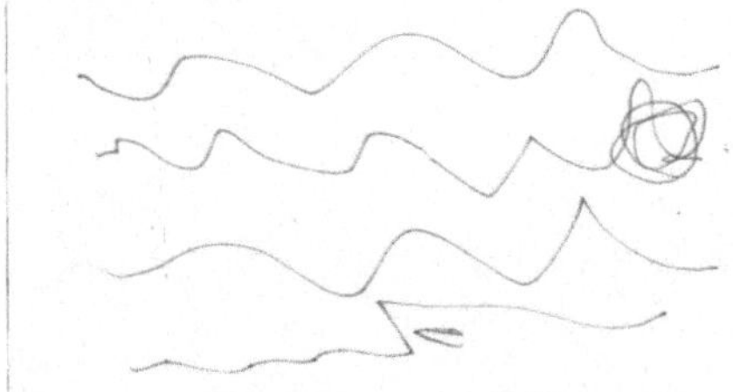

Figure 4.10. A child scribbles from left to right and top to bottom, reflecting the directionality of writing in English.

Figure 4.11. Children write using letter-like forms (symbols that look similar to letters).

Letter-like forms and random letter strings. Children then begin writing with forms that look like letters but aren't quite letters. We call these *letter-like forms*. They might also add in other symbols and numbers.

As children's fine motor skills continue to develop, they will learn how to form letters of the alphabet. Children will come to understand the alphabet as a distinct symbol system and their writing will include entirely or mainly letters. It is very common to see young children write with the letters in their name, repeated over and over. For example, at 3 years old, Macie writes a story about a princess, seen in Figure 4.12.

Notice how the letters are made up of letters from her name. If you looked at this writing sample out of context, without knowing Macie was writing about a princess, you might think she wrote the word *mama*. But Macie's writing does not yet attend to the connection between the words she says and the letters she writes.

Figure 4.12. Young children may write using letters from their own name. While it looks like Macie has written the word *mama*, she explains that she has written a story about a princess.

Salient and beginning sounds. Another exciting development happens when children begin connecting spoken sounds with letters. In other words, when they understand the alphabetic principle. Children will begin writing with *estimated spelling*, where they are writing letters based on the sounds that are present in the message they are communicating. At first, they will write with sounds that are *salient*, or prominent, as they say a word or sentence. For example, if a child is trying to

About the Term *Estimated Spelling*

We use the term *estimated spelling* instead of *invented spelling* to describe young children's writing. After children have grasped the alphabetic principle, they actively use their sound-letter knowledge to estimate the spelling of the word. There is a logic to this and it is not arbitrary, as the word *invented* might imply (Read 1971).

Some believe children must always spell words correctly. They may worry that children's knowledge of the word's incorrect spelling will "stick." However, research finds just the opposite. When young children estimate the spellings of words, it actually supports their later spelling development (Ouellette, Sénéchal, & Haley 2013). Estimating spelling provides a context for children to strengthen their phonemic segmentation (see Chapter 3), consider how specific sounds are represented by letters, and develop greater fluency with letter formation. We recommend that educators let go of any concerns about conventional spellings at this early point in children's development and encourage children to use what they are learning to estimate spellings.

write the word *elbow*, they might write the letter *l* or *o* because those are the sounds that are most prominent. In this case, the letter names *l* and *o* in the word can be heard in the word *elbow.* Often the most salient sound to a child is the first sound in a word.

Beginning and ending sounds. The next step in development of spelling is the ability to write the beginning and ending sounds in a word or syllable. The ability to represent the first sound means the child

- Has acquired important concepts of print, such as directionality
- Understands the alphabetic principle
- Can segment the initial sound in a word
- Knows several sound–letter relationships
- Has learned to form a number of letters

If children can do more than this, that is great too. For example, a child writing the word *cold* by writing *CD* has learned to represent the ending as well as the initial sound. Later in development, that same child might write more sounds they hear in the word, including vowel sounds (e.g., *COD*).

Children may experience frustration because they are not always able to read back what they have written. This is because they now understand that there is a specific message they were trying to share. Writing also becomes very labor intensive for young children when they are

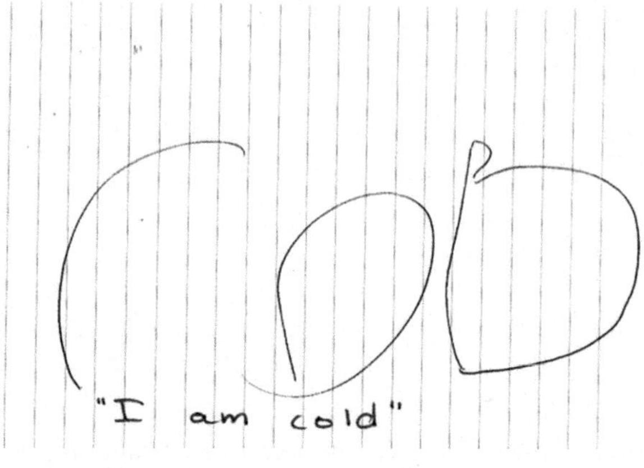

Figure 4.13. Children may represent a word using several sounds. This child told her mother that her message was "I am cold."

RESEARCH NOTE

Names Are Special

Often, the first string of letters children learn to write is their first name (Ferreiro & Teberosky 1982). Names are special to us and are a great teaching tool to learn about the names and sounds of letters of the alphabet (Levin et al. 2005). Children often see their own names as labels in the environment both at home and in the classroom. Most preschool teachers emphasize name recognition and writing.

Children typically learn to write their names at a much more rapid rate than they learn to write other words (Levin et al. 2005). By the end of preschool, many children can write their first names accurately. They may also be able to write names of friends or family members (for example, *mommy*). A child who can write names may give the impression that they know the alphabetic principle, but they might still be learning this important concept. It is important to look at a variety of writing to understand children's spelling development.

Figure 4.14. Children learn to write their own names and names of friends and family members.

estimating spellings because they are practicing their knowledge of sounds and letters and how they go together. This is hard work at first. Support from teachers can help children's writing and reading to grow (Ouellette, Sénéchal, & Haley 2013).

Handwriting

Handwriting is another area of writing that begins to develop in early childhood. With adult support, young children learn to hold writing tools (such as pencils) and make the shapes of letters. As an educator, your focus is on helping children learn how to form letters and not on perfect penmanship.

Why does handwriting matter? When young children can write letters without undue effort, coupled with their growing spelling ability, they are more able to focus on what they want to communicate through their writing (composing). Children usually don't reach this goal in preschool, but experiences in early childhood can lay the groundwork for handwriting development. By the end of preschool, most children will start to learn to make the shape of letters, but fluent and efficient letter formation is not an expectation until the early elementary years. Most important, when you teach children to make letter shapes, you help children connect the shapes with the letter name and letter sound.

Showing

Educators can show or demonstrate writing throughout the day. Two important strategies are creating class books and incorporating writing into transitions.

Creating Class Books

A wonderful way to explain and show children about writing is to create books as a class. Each child can contribute a page to the book either by dictating their words to a teacher and drawing or by drawing and using estimated spelling to write words independently. Young children love to create books. They get excited about becoming authors, and the ideas for what to write about are unlimited.

The following are some ideas for making class books:

- **About Our Class.** Create a book that includes a photo of each child and invite the child to share something about themselves to help friends get to know them.
- **Your Birthday Book.** Create a book for each child on their birthday. Each child in the classroom can contribute a drawing and words wishing their classmate well.
- **Our Neighborhood.** Take a walk around the neighborhood near your school. Invite children to observe, draw, and write about what they see. Consider taking photographs to add to the book.
- **Our Field Trip.** Visit a museum, a farm, a zoo, a park, or any other field trip that you typically take as a class. Invite each child to contribute a page about what they saw or learned on the trip.
- **Our Observations of ______.** If you grow a plant in the classroom, have a tree outside, or even a class pet, invite children to observe the plant or pet regularly and draw and write about what they see. Consider making this a class job and inviting a different child to add a page each week. Children (and adults) will find it fascinating to look back and see how living things grow and change over the course of a year.
- **People in Our School Community.** Invite other people who work in the building where your school or child care center is housed for a visit. Children can prepare questions to ask them about their job. Based on what they learn, children can create a book about the people or about their occupations.
- **We Learned About ______.** For any topic that you are studying or learning about, invite children to draw and write about what they have learned.
- **Create a personalized version of a familiar picture book**. For example, make a class version of the book *Freight Train*, by Donald Crews. Children can add their own drawings of trains and write or tell their own words.

Children can share these books with audiences outside of their classroom, such as families, members of the community, other classes, and school staff.

Show children how you approach writing and draw their attention to the actions and ideas that are most relevant to their understanding and development. As needed, you can periodically show a child how to form a particular letter they want to write, although transitions are probably not a time for tracing or copying.

TRANSITIONS

Integrating Writing into Transitions

One purpose of writing is to remind us of important information. Children and teachers can create texts that provide reminders during transitions, such as

- Labels as reminders of where things go at cleanup time
- Signs as reminders of specific actions during transitions ("Use walking feet to be safe")
- Lists to remind children of what they plan to do during the next portion of the day ("1. Puzzles, 2. Sensory Table, 3. Book Nook")
- Reminder notes about supplies needed ("Please buy more blue paper")
- Notes to remind children and family members about events ("Remember to talk about our trip to the farmers' market")

KEY PRACTICES

Designing and Including

Designing as a key practice includes the intentional planning and preparation of the classroom, schedule, and materials to provide a rich variety of learning experiences. **Including** is a key practice essential to welcoming every child to the learning experience, ensuring equal access to learning, and fostering respectful and affirming relationships.

Designing

Including authentic writing materials and practices from homes and community settings is important for designing culturally relevant and sustaining early childhood classrooms. These expand beyond what commercially produced materials, books, posters, and other classroom materials provide, which have been shown to overrepresent White English-speaking children (Souto-Manning 2013; Souto-Manning et al. 2018). This simple practice of ensuring that children's experiences in their homes and communities are present in the early childhood classroom communicates belonging.

There are many ways to ensure that writing materials and practices present in early childhood classrooms mirror children's home and community knowledge and practices. At the same time, teachers can ensure that children learn from and about writing practices that are different from their own. Encourage children to bring writing from their homes and community settings as well as share family stories. In this section, we offer a few additional ideas and invite you to ask the following: Is the writing in my classroom representative of the children, families, and

Informal Inventory: Writing in the Early Childhood Environment

The following questions are helpful as you reflect on the writing in your classroom:

- What writing do I see?
- What do the walls tell me about writing in my classroom?
- What do the books and other written materials in my classroom tell me?
- Whose writing is represented?
- Whose writing is missing or not as prominently represented?
- How is the writing in my classroom honoring children's cultures, language practices, and identities?
- Is the diversity of writing in my classroom characteristic of the composition of the preschool/center and the larger community where it is located? As a whole? With regard to race, gender, and language?
- Do any written materials in my classroom present or center on privileged positions?

These questions can help you engage in taking an inventory to assess the adequacy of your classroom's written materials for facilitating the learning of diverse children, especially those who have historically been marginalized and excluded.

communities it serves? Does the writing here attend to the broader society in which it is located? How do I know?

Sometimes, educators perceive their classrooms to be much more inclusive and diverse than they are. The trouble is that when a teacher perceives their classroom as diverse, they are less likely to work to create a more inclusive, diverse, and welcoming classroom. What to do? We suggest an informal inventory. Building on Souto-Manning and Martell's (2016) invitation to look around and consider what story your classroom tells and how you can rewrite it, we invite you to notice and note what books, labels, and other written materials are present in your classroom.

Writing from Home and Community

Educators can encourage children to bring writing from home (recipes, grocery lists, notes, packages of food to be recycled, empty hair products with written instructions) and from the community where they live (fliers, advertisements, receipts, coupons, to-go menus). This is an easy yet powerful way to ensure that children see the purposes of writing and are exposed to different kinds of writing.

Written text from communities can illustrate multiple purposes and forms of writing. This variety can enrich the classroom texts, ensuring representativeness and diversity. For example, through recipes, food boxes, and hair products (well-washed containers), children can learn about procedural writing. Through advertisements for groceries, they may learn about the many labels for particular foods. Through receipts and coupons, they will notice the sorting of numbers and letters. These different kinds of writing can be immersed in multiple areas of the classroom. For example, a housekeeping area may include grocery lists, a restaurant area may include to-go menus in various named languages, and a library area may include labeled bins with books.

You may invite children to take pictures of print they see around their neighborhood and on their way to school. This collection will provide a variety of written materials and representations authentic to young children, representing multiple family artifacts and communities. Here are a few examples:

- In a preschool classroom, a teacher engaged children in developing an ABC book about their preschool. Because they were located in New York City, they used the book *ABC NYC: A Book About Seeing New York City*, by Joanne Dugan, as a mentor text, which ignited children's imagination for composing their own book. Because many children in the class spoke Spanish at home, the teacher also read *Just In Case: A Trickster Tale and Spanish Alphabet Book*, by Yuyi Morales.
- In a Head Start classroom, children took pictures on their way to the park (where they had recess), creating a written story with audio narration that they shared with families. Family members reported on how surprised the children were to know that their families knew about what they saw on their way to the playground. This activity extended to family members who encouraged their children to note print in their own environment.
- Everyday objects can serve as points of access to the daily experiences and the world in which young children live (Pahl & Rowsell 2019). Objects from children's homes and communities can support literacy learning when teachers purposefully and intentionally use these objects to access family stories and intergenerational tales. To foster this practice, teachers may use a family photo, heirloom, or recipe to support the development of stories. Building on the idea that every object can help tell a story, a Head Start teacher invited 3- to 5-year-old children to bring an object from home or from the community that tells an important story. In preparation, she read *What Can You Do with a Paleta?/¿Qué puedes hacer con una paleta?* by Carmen Tafolla, illustrated by Magaly Morales, and *This Is the Rope: A Story from the Great Migration*, by Jacqueline Woodson, illustrated by James Ransome. In doing so, the teacher deemphasized the show-and-tell nature of bringing something from home, instead focusing on a paleta (popsicle) and a jump rope. Then, she invited the children to create a museum, labeling the objects and telling a story about them. They even created an audio guide for their museum and a brochure (just like the ones they had encountered in the American Museum of Natural History).
- In a preschool classroom, a parent played the oboe and invited the children to make a double reed from straw, an activity that helped the children understand the relationship between sound and vibration. The children wrote about how to make a double reed, writing down steps using drawings and other symbols individually and then composing a class text, dictating the steps to their teacher. They then shared the writing with their families.
- A Head Start class went to a recycling station where the uncle of one of the children worked. There they learned about the importance of recycling and reusing. They created labels for the trash cans in their classrooms, repurposing some of the cans as recycling bins. In doing so, they understood the meaning of labels.

Family funds of knowledge and community cultural wealth are also great sources of stories and materials for books. Educators can also create space for family stories, composing family books that narrate special, funny, or everyday experiences as well as special events. These can then be recorded in writing and collected in a family stories book. In a toddler classroom, grandparents and other community elders can pass down songs to be written in books and recorded for children's listening. Teachers can draw children's attention to the text, supporting associations between oral and written words.

Teachers can also invite young children to write about small moments from their homes and communities, using writing to document, remember, and produce knowledge. For example, they can write down what they hear when they go to sleep, and the children's writing can be put together in a multilingual book featuring every child, that reads as follows:

When I go to sleep, I hear . . .

- *Buenas noches, mi amor.*
- *Good night, sleep tight.*
- *Wen-wen-wen* (the sound of an ambulance).
- *Boa noite, durma bem.*
- *I love you a bushel and a peck.*
- *Night, night.*

This practice of collecting authentic writing from children's homes is likely to include multiple ways of communicating across several named languages.

Educators can also encourage children to write letters to family members who live far away. Children can write to tell the teacher about events and happenings to their families. Creating a board where reminders are written in the classroom is another great way to demonstrate the purpose and power of writing.

Including

Writing can communicate inclusion and belonging. Inclusive early childhood teachers envision, plan, and build bridges among young children's interests, expertise, experiences, individualities, and written language. Teachers identify the strengths and interests of children, unveiling what motivates them, then representing and including these strengths and interests in the writing present in an early childhood classroom. Teachers employ written language, writing, written materials, and artifacts to communicate "You belong here" and "I see you." There are many ways to include writing in the early childhood classroom.

Inclusion and Writing

Here we discuss four ideas for attending to inclusion as it pertains to writing.

1. **Use words from home languages.** At age 1, Mariana's son used words in Portuguese and sign symbols to communicate. He used *água* for *water, mais* for *more*, and the sign symbol for *all done*. He used *papai* (which sounds like "popeye") to say "daddy"; his peers soon learned that *pai* (pronounced "pie") or *papai* were his way of saying "dad" or "daddy." He used *bye* in English. His teacher wrote down keywords he used, both in the language in which the word was spoken and phonemically. While his teacher was not fluent in Portuguese, uttering familiar words was

not only a way to build connection with him but also a way to validate his communication. Eventually, he learned to speak in the named languages of English, Portuguese, and Spanish, attending (mostly) to the conventions of those named languages. His teacher's effort to honor and build on his communication were extremely important for his development as a multilingual learner. As educators, it is important to commit to honoring and affirming children's language practices. Writing serves to include children when it honors children's communication. Just as this toddler teacher, you too can write down words familiar to an infant or toddler and use those words to foster a more inclusive classroom.

2. **Develop the motor skills needed for writing.** Building hand and finger muscle strength helps support children's writing development. This happens through a variety of play activities. Many opportunities for young children to develop fine motor skills take place in the context of the toddler classroom. For example, working with playdough and finger painting—as well as designing opportunities for children to pick up objects of multiple sizes—are activities that foster young children's fine motor development. Tools that allow children to pick up sand from the sand table or toy fish from a water table also support the development of these small muscles. Additionally, having an array of toddler-appropriate materials for writing, drawing, and painting will ensure that young children have plenty of opportunities for building the fine motor skills eventually needed for what we call writing. As children start to engage in writing, honor and include all early forms of writing, including marks, scribbles, drawings, and more.

   Children's fine motor skills can also happen through the intentional use of touch screens. A cleanup routine can become an important way of engaging toddlers in grasping and releasing toys and other objects of varying sizes and shapes. Infant teachers can engage in fingerplays. Embed pathways to develop fine motor skills, whether buttoning a coat, picking up a Cheerio, or putting away blocks. Writing development is at work when children practice the fine motor skills that make writing possible.

3. **Value estimated spelling and include ways of writing from across named languages.** Often children's initial writings will include letters, sounds, and assumptions that are influenced and shaped by culture. For example, in English the syllables *da da* may refer to dad or father, yet in Portuguese, *dá dá* signals "give me, give me." To write *da da* (or simply *da*) may then mean "give me." While it is impossible to know every language, educators can honor children's language backgrounds, affirming their practices. Educators can work to understand the logic and meaning of children's writing, whether in symbols, such as letters, or "art notes" or drawings (Dyson 1989).

Figure 4.15. A child's art note.

   Figure 4.15 shows an art note composed by Ju 据, a Chinese immigrant child in Early Head Start after her teacher read *Brown Bear, Brown Bear, What Do You See?* by Bill Martin Jr. and Eric Carle.

   Although this page may appear to be simply scribbles, when considered with knowledge of the picture book that inspired this child, it is easy to see how this child drew the blue horse on the bottom left corner, the purple cat on the upper left corner, and brought the green frog to life as it jumped across the page. This consideration of the child's work in context allowed the teacher to assess the child's understanding, even when the child was not yet expressing her comprehension orally.

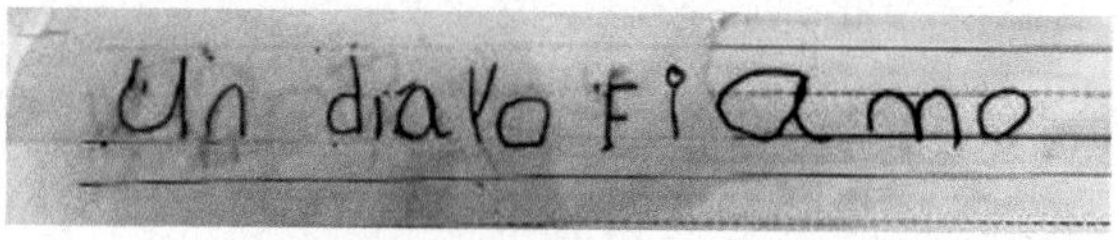

Figure 4.16. This child composes a meaningful sentence from English and Spanish: ***Un día, yo fui al mall.***

Valuing spelling estimations across named languages can support multilingual children's writing. In Figure 4.16, 4-year-old Alicia wrote *Un día, yo fui al mall*, composing a meaningful sentence from English and Spanish.

Alicia shows us how she brought together the word *mall* (mo) with *Un día, yo fui al* (Un dia yo fi a).

Alicia's writing demonstrates how children can translanguage by combining words from more than one named language in the same sentence as well as translanguaging within words.

When Alicia's teacher introduced the book *¡Si, Se Puede!/Yes, We Can! Janitor Strike in L.A.*, by Diana Cohn, illustrated by Francisco Delgado, the teacher pointed at an illustration of a woman mopping the floor of what appeared to be an office and asked, "What is she doing?" Alicia answered excitedly, "Esta mopeando." Although the word *mopeando* may not be the expected word, it is important to understand that the child is knowledgeably bringing named languages together, drawing on her full communicative repertoire. Instead of using *trapeando* (a Spanish translation of *mopping*), she combined *mop* (in English) with the verb tense from Spanish (*-eando*). This instance of intraword translanguaging offers an important window into Alicia's knowledge of languages and how they work. This practice does not demonstrate a lack of knowledge; it shows multilingualism at work. As discussed previously, children do not automatically separate their vocabulary and other communicative resources into distinct language categories as adults do; this is something they learn as they develop as literacy learners and communicators. These are all expected milestones in the literacy development of multilingual children.

4. **Learn children's names.** When working with young children to support their development as writers, start with meaningful concepts, such as names. As explained earlier, working with children to write names is an important focus in early childhood. Researchers (Kohli & Solórzano 2012; Souto-Manning 2007) have shown the importance of learning how to say children's names as their family members and loved ones say it. To include children, it is essential that we do not deem names to be wrong; they are each unique. Ensure that however a name is written, it is pronounced in alignment with how the child, their family, and community pronounce it. This is essential to communicate inclusion and belonging.

For example, the name *Tara* can be pronounced with "air" or with "ahr" following the *T*. It is important to note that sound–letter associations (explored in Chapter 3) that defy English-language conventions apply to names as well. For example, *Niamh* may be pronounced "nee-ev" (two syllables) and *Xiomara* may be pronounced

> Take the time to learn how to pronounce children's names, spell them accurately, and show respect for their importance to children and families.

"see-oh-MAR-uh." At times, the same name can be pronounced multiple ways; *Xavier* can be pronounced "ha-vee-AIR," "zay-vee-er," or "EX-zay-vee-er." Our advice? Take the time to learn how to pronounce children's names, spell them accurately, and show respect for their importance to children and families.

KEY PRACTICES

Engaging and Explaining

Engaging children with early writing is a key practice that happens throughout the day during planned activities, daily routines, and play. Through the key teaching practice of **Explaining**, teachers provide support for learning to write.

Engaging

To encourage young children to write, provide them with access to writing materials and tools in the classroom so that they can engage in writing throughout the day. These materials might include the following:

- Materials for infants, toddlers, and preschoolers to strengthen their hands and develop fine motor control
- Magnetic boards and other safe materials that children can use to make marks before they have learned not to put markers, pencils, and paint in their mouths
- Puppets and felt boards to support storytelling
- Writing tools, such as pencils, markers, crayons, colored pencils, and chalk
- Writing utensils, different materials to write on, and a handheld alphabet chart in a classroom writing center
- Writing materials included in other parts of the classroom, such as pencils and graph paper on clipboards in the block area
- Digital options and devices for preschoolers to write and document what they see, such as tablets to draw on or to use to make audio recordings of their ideas and digital cameras or tablets for children to document what they see

These materials will lead to writing experiences that happen in meaningful ways. Name writing can be used to sign into a dental office play center or to sign artwork. Encourage children to write more than their names. They can write grocery lists in a housekeeping center, take orders in the classroom restaurant, write stories in the writing center, make labels in a block center (as well as signs asking janitors and other adults not to put blocks away), and use observational journals in a science center.

Figure 4.17. This child decides to write the whole alphabet on a white board.

Teach Children How to Use Writing Materials

Giving children access to writing materials can increase children's engagement with these materials (Neuman & Roskos 1992). But it is even more powerful for children's learning when teachers support children's use of these materials (Neuman & Roskos 1993). Show children how to use the materials. For example, during dramatic play, you might take the role of the veterinarian first and demonstrate how to write a prescription for medicine for an animal and take notes on a medical chart. Then the child can take on the role, and you could fade out of the center while children swap roles with each other.

Include Writing in Play

As children understand that writing is one way to convey messages, teachers can encourage children by inviting them to add writing into their drawings and as part of dramatic play. This might even include digital forms of writing (Rowe et al. 2021). For example, Figure 4.18 shows a drawing that 3-year-old Ella made during play time. When her teacher asked her to tell more about the picture, she said, "That's me," while pointing to her name and the smaller figure. Pointing to the larger figure, she continued, "And that's Daddy giving me a hug." She incorporated writing her name into her artwork.

Figure 4.18. It is common for young children to reverse the direction of symbols.

Figure 4.19 shows a sign that says *opin* (open). After visiting a museum, children in a classroom of 4-year-olds made their own art museum by hanging up the artwork they were making. When they were done taping their artwork to the wall, they asked their teacher for help to make a sign to show their peers that their museum was open. Their teachers supported their play by helping them to stretch out the word and figure out which letters they could use to write this word.

Figure 4.19. Children use a sign to show that their art museum is open.

As children play, it is common for them to want to include forms of writing that they see in their everyday lives and naturally fit into dramatic play. These may include

- Invitations
- Letters
- Menus
- Order forms
- Maps

- Instructions
- Reminders
- Signs

Teachers can help children by supporting their writing during play. For example, toddlers may dictate words for teachers to write and older children may need help to stretch out words and represent their sounds.

Use Scaffolded Writing During Play

While some young children may write independently, many children benefit from teachers using the *scaffolded writing technique* during play (Bodrova & Leong 1998). Teachers scaffold children's writing in the following ways:

1. The teacher helps the child to orally speak the message they want to write.
2. The teacher encourages the child to repeat the message several times so they remember what they planned to write.
3. The teacher or child can draw a line to create an area on the paper for each word that the child wants to write. A highlighter could also be used to make an area for each word.
4. The teacher and child point to each line or highlighted area while repeating the message several times.
5. The child writes one "word" of the message on each line. For toddlers, this might be a scribble or letter-like form on each line. For preschoolers, the teacher can help children stretch the word and listen for sounds to represent with letters.
6. The teacher and the child "read" the message back together.
7. The teacher and child use the message for its intended purpose (for example, in the dramatic play in which the child was involved).

Explaining

As part of supporting children's writing development, there are opportunities across the day for teachers to explain how writing works. This includes explaining about composing, spelling, and handwriting to help children understand why and how these aspects of writing work.

Teachers can explain and show as they compose:

"We are making a book about your family. This is a picture of your grandma. Would you like me to write *Grandma* next to her picture?"

"I'm going to write your name on masking tape and put it on your water bottle. Then we'll know which one is yours."

"I'm going to write a reminder to myself to bring in the seeds we want to plant tomorrow. I'm writing *Bring in seeds.*"

"Lilah says she thinks that the seed will grow in the closet. So, I am writing *The seed will grow* next to Lilah's name, and I am drawing a picture of a seed with a little sprout growing out of it."

Teachers can explain and show as they spell:

"I'm writing the word *seed* right now. Sssssseed. What sound do you hear at the beginning of the word *ssssssseed*? Yes. It's the /s/ sound. Which letter will I write for the /s/ sound? Children are saying I should write the letter *s*. So, I am going to write *s* for the /s/ sound in *seed*."

Teachers can explain and show how to make letters:

"You want to write the letter *B* for *Brody.* Let me show you on my whiteboard so you can see how to make this letter and then you can try it. Start at the top and draw a line down. (*Teacher demonstrates.*) Then go back to the top and make a half circle that looks like a bump on the line and then we make another bump. So you can remember that it's a line with two bumps. Okay. Now you try."

Interactive Writing

There are many opportunities to support children's writing by explaining and showing children how writing works. This includes that writing is important for conveying meaning, purposes for particular types of writing, directionality of writing, and specific sound–letter relationships. One way to engage children in writing is through *interactive writing*. Research finds that interactive writing can support literacy development (Hall et al. 2014). For example, when 3- to 5-year-old children engaged in interactive writing in their Head Start classroom, their alphabet knowledge grew more than that of the children who experienced typical early literacy instruction.

In interactive writing, teachers work with a small group of children to compose and write together, helping children to contribute based on their individual knowledge and skills. Here are some common steps in interactive writing:

1. **Children and teacher determine the message**. For example, in one classroom of 4-year-olds, children were frustrated because blocks were hard to find when they were put back on the wrong shelf. With teacher support, they decided to write a message to remind classmates about this. They discussed the message and agreed that they wanted to write, *Please put the blocks back on the right shelf.*
2. **The teacher plans a teaching point that is appropriate for the children in the group.** In this case, the teacher plans to work on segmentation of words and explaining to children that sounds are represented by letters.
3. **Working with one word at a time, children work with their teacher to stretch out each word, listening for sounds in the word.** For example, after stretching out *please* ("plllleaeaeasssse") and repeating the /p/ sound at the beginning, children could hear the /p/ sound at the beginning of the word as well as some of the other sounds in the word.

4. **Children take turns representing the sounds in words with letters and take turns writing the letters they know.** For example, Clara took a turn to write the letter *p* at the beginning of the first line. The teacher showed Clara how to make a *p* on her whiteboard when Clara couldn't remember the shape. Then Clara wrote her *p* at the beginning of the first line.
5. **This process continues with the teacher helping by "filling in" words and sounds that are hard to represent.** As the teacher models writing, it is important to explain why as well as show how so that children know what the teacher is doing. After the children worked to represent sounds for *please* and *put*, their teacher said, "I'm going to write the word *the* on this third line. I wrote a *t* and an *h* because together they make the /th/ sound and then an /e/, which makes the /uh/ sound in this word."
6. **The teacher and children read the entire message and children use the message in a meaningful way.** After reading back their message, children added drawings to show putting blocks on the correct shelves, and then they hung their sign in the block area.

KEY PRACTICES

Observing and Responding

Observing children is a key practice that informs teachers' understanding of children's learning—where they are now in their development and what they are ready to learn next. What teachers learn through observation will guide them in effectively **Responding** to children in ways that support learning.

Observing

Watching as young children develop early writing is exciting for early childhood educators. Children are so proud when they see their words written down, when they can tell about a picture they have created, or when they can first write their own name. Observing children's development also helps educators to understand what learning to scaffold next.

Educators should not be concerned about children writing letters in reverse in the birth-to-age-5 years. In this age range, writing letters in this way is developmentally expected and not a sign of a learning difficulty or difference (see discussion of directionality of print in Chapter 2 and Figure 4.18).

	Age	Literacy Development: Milestones in Early Writing
Infants	Birth–12 months	• Begins to develop fine motor skills (for example, picking up smaller and smaller objects).
Toddlers	1–3 years	• Makes marks on paper using a variety of tools (markers, crayons, and so on). • Asks adults to scribe for them. ("Can you write *happy birthday* right here?"). • Pretends to write using scribbles or letter-like shapes. • Tells about their drawings or artwork.
Preschoolers	3–5 years	• Writes own name. • Participates in interactive and scaffolded writing opportunities. • Writes words using letter-like symbols (early preschool) or real letters (later in preschool). • Writes to share messages that are meaningful to the child, including labeling drawings to add information (such as making a menu for a pretend restaurant or writing a *d* next to a picture of their dad). • Writes to align with the type of text being created (child might ask to make a card that is folded or to staple multiple papers together to make a book). • Asks adult to write dictated words (for example, asks adult to write *I am playing with Elliot* below a picture drawn by the child). • Writes with estimated spelling (such as writing *R, RN*, or *RAN* for *rain*).

Table 4.1. Milestones in Early Writing Development

Responding

After observing children's writing, teachers can respond to help them take the next step in their understanding of how to be a writer. The more you know about children's understandings, the better you can build on what children know to support next steps. Remember that the way teachers figure out what children understand about writing is by watching what they do, listening to what they say, and looking carefully at their written artifacts. Children's drawing and writing attempts help teachers to figure out what they already know and how to support their writing development.

When you observe the child . . .	You may respond by . . .
Infants	
Picking up objects.	Providing a lot of opportunities for infants to practice fine motor skills by playing with and picking up objects (for example toys, foods, utensils).
Toddlers	
Drawing pictures or scribbles.	Asking children to tell you about their work. Affirming children's messages and inviting them to tell more.
Making marks on paper using drawing/ writing tools.	Providing a lot of tools for children to explore with (finger paint, paintbrushes, markers, crayons, pencils, paper and scissors, digital drawing and writing tools, and so on).
Preschoolers	
Writing with seemingly random letters.	Remembering that these letters are likely not random, because they are usually familiar letters in the child's name repeated over and over. They do not yet connect with the sounds of what children are trying to say. Helping the child to see that letters and sounds connect by displaying the child's or a friend's name and drawing attention to the beginning letter and sound in the name.
Writing with estimated spelling (for example, writing *B* for *bat*).	Validating this important understanding that words and sounds we say can be written down. Helping them to hear other sounds in words by stretching out the word (for example, *bat* as "baaaattttt") with the focus on the final sound of the word, encouraging them to write *BT* for *bat*. Teaching sound-letter relationships (see Chapter 3).

Table 4.2. Observing and Responding

Moving Forward

Observing and supporting children's writing development is one of the most exciting aspects of early childhood literacy education. You get to see concrete artifacts of children's development right before your eyes!

Among other things, you foster children's writing development when you

- **Know** how young children's writing develops with respect to composition, spelling, and handwriting. Value each child's ways of communicating through print—drawing, scribbling, letter-like forms, random letter strings, representation of single sounds from each word or syllable, or representation of multiple sounds within each word.
- **Show** the importance and meaning of writing by inviting children to bring in authentic writing from home and from the communities where they live.

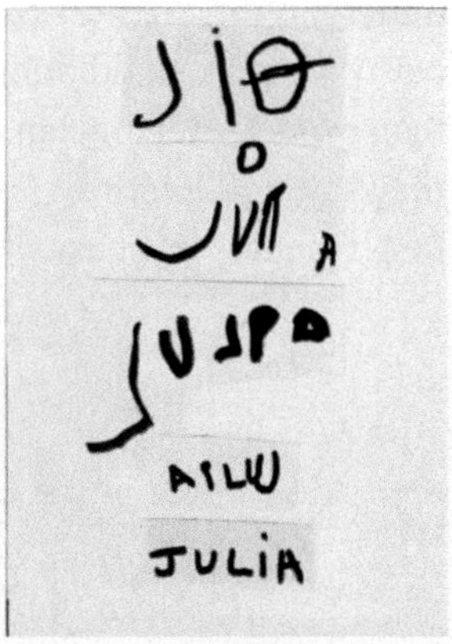

Figure 4.20. A young child's progress in writing their name, *Julia*.

- **Design** writing experiences for children by conducting ongoing inventories of your classroom to ensure it includes a lot of writing from children themselves and writing developed in collaboration with children. Provide writing utensils and materials to write on throughout the classroom, in addition to in a writing center.
- **Include** all children by incorporating children's language practices and repertoires, encouraging and welcoming writing reflecting any and all of these language practices and repertoires. Recognize that writing with estimated spelling supports, rather than detracts from, children's later ability to spell words conventionally.
- **Engage** children in writing by developing class books that become part of the classroom library and are shared with audiences outside of the classroom. Use the scaffolded writing technique and use writing in meaningful ways during planning and transition times.
- **Explain**, model, and engage children in collaborative writing for authentic purposes, such as writing a thank-you letter to a field trip host or sharing information with another class. Use the interactive writing technique with children regularly.
- **Observe** children's writing and respond in ways that validate what they have done and support their continued development.
- **Respond** to observations by supporting the development of children's fine motor skills, using scaffolded writing to support children individually in writing messages important to them and more.

Considering new ideas about how to support resourceful writers will take time. We recommend revisiting this chapter several times to incorporate the information and ideas into your classroom. We also recommend selecting a few ideas to try at a time. For example, you might focus first on implementing scaffolded writing in your classroom. Use professional reflection and support from colleagues to refine your practice in that area. Then move on to implementing the next set of ideas. We are excited to think about all of the wonderful writing children in your classroom will do!

References

Bereiter, C., & M. Scardamalia. 1987. *The Psychology of Written Composition*. Mahwah, NJ: Lawrence Erlbaum Associates.

Berninger, V.W. 2009. "Highlights of Programmatic, Interdisciplinary Research on Writing." *Learning Disabilities Research and Practice* 24: 68–79.

Berninger, V.W., & H.L. Swanson. 1994. "Modifying Hayes and Flower's Model of Skilled Writing to Explain Beginning and Developing Writing." In *Children's Writing: Toward a Process Theory of Development of Skilled Writing*, ed. E. Butterfield, 57–81. Stamford, CT: JAI Press.

Bodrova, E., & D.J. Leong. 1998. "Scaffolding Emergent Writing in the Zone of Proximal Development." *Literacy Teaching and Learning* 3: 1–18.

Cabell, S.Q., L.S. Tortorelli, & H.K. Gerde. 2013. "How Do I Write . . . ? Scaffolding Preschoolers' Early Writing Skills." *The Reading Teacher* 66: 650–59.

Dyson, A.H. 1989. "The Space/Time Travels of Story Writers." *Language Arts* 66 (3): 330–40.

Ferreiro, E., & A. Teberosky. 1982. *Literacy Before Schooling*. Portsmouth, NH: Heinemann.

Graham, S. 2018. "A Revised Writer(s)-Within-Community Model of Writing." *Educational Psychologist* 53 (4): 258–79.

Graham, S., & M.A. Hebert. 2010. *Writing to Read: Evidence for How Writing Can Improve Reading*. Carnegie Corporation Time to Act Report. Washington, DC: Alliance for Excellent Education.

Graham, S., & M.A. Hebert. 2011. "Writing to Read: A Meta-Analysis of the Impact of Writing and Writing Instruction on Reading." *Harvard Educational Review* 81 (4): 710–44.

Hall, A.H., M.D. Toland, J. Grisham-Brown, & S. Graham. 2014. "Exploring Interactive Writing as an Effective Practice for Increasing Head Start Students' Alphabet Knowledge Skills." *Early Childhood Education Journal* 42: 423–30.

Kaderavek, J.N., S.Q. Cabell, & L.M. Justice. 2009. "Early Writing and Spelling Development." In *Emergent Literacy and Language Development: Promoting Learning in Early Childhood*, ed. P.M. Rhyner, 104–52. New York: Guilford Press.

Kim, Y.S., & C. Schatschneider. 2016. "Expanding the Developmental Models of Writing." *Journal of Educational Psychology* 109 (1): 35–50.

Kohli, R., & D.G. Solórzano. 2012. "Teachers, Please Learn Our Names! Racial Microaggressions and the K–12 Classroom." *Race Ethnicity and Education* 15 (4): 441–62.

Levin, I., A. Both-De Vries, D. Aram, & A. Bus. 2005. "Writing Starts with Own Name Writing: From Scribbling to Conventional Spelling in Israeli and Dutch Children." *Applied Psycholinguistics* 26 (3): 463–77.

National Early Literacy Panel. 2008. *Developing Early Literacy: Report of the National Early Literacy Panel.* Washington, DC: National Institute for Literacy.

Neuman, S.B., & K. Roskos. 1992. "Literacy Objects as Cultural Tools: Effects on Children's Literacy Behaviors in Play." *Reading Research Quarterly* 27: 202–25.

Neuman, S.B., & K. Roskos. 1993. "Access to Print for Children of Poverty: Differential Effects of Adult Mediation and Literacy-Enriched Play Settings on Environmental and Functional Print Tasks." *American Educational Research Journal* 30: 95–122.

Ouellette, G., M. Sénéchal, & A. Haley. 2013. "Guiding Children's Invented Spellings: A Gateway into Literacy Learning. *The Journal of Experimental Education* 81: 261–79.

Owocki, G., & Y. Goodman. 2002. *Kidwatching: Documenting Children's Literacy Development.* Portsmouth, NH: Heinemann.

Pahl, K., & J. Rowsell. 2019. *Artifactual Literacies: Every Object Tells a Story.* New York: Teachers College Press.

Read, C. 1971. "Pre-school Children's Knowledge of English Phonology." *Harvard Educational Review* 41: 1–34.

Rowe, D.W., & M.E. Miller. 2016. "Designing for Diverse Classrooms: Using iPads and Digital Cameras to Compose eBooks with Emergent Bilingual/Biliterate Four-Year-Olds." *Journal of Early Childhood Literacy* 16 (4): 425–72.

Souto-Manning, M. 2007. "Honoring Children's Names and, Therefore, Their Identities." *School Talk* 12 (3): 1–2.

Souto-Manning, M. 2013. *Multicultural Teaching in the Early Childhood Classroom: Approaches, Strategies, and Tools.* New York: Teachers College Press.

Souto-Manning, M., C.L. Llerena, J. Martell, A.S. Maguire, & A. Arce-Boardman. 2018. *No More Culturally Irrelevant Teaching.* Portsmouth, NH: Heinemann.

Souto-Manning, M., & J. Martell. 2016. *Reading, Writing, and Talk: Inclusive Teaching Strategies for Diverse Learners, K–2.* New York: Teachers College Press.

Stadler, M.A., & G.C. Ward. 2005. "Supporting the Narrative Development of Young Children." *Early Childhood Education Journal* 33: 73–80.

Text Comprehenders

When my (coauthor Nell Duke's) daughter was about 6 months old, I read to her *The Very Busy Spider*, by Eric Carle. As its title suggests, in this story a spider is very busy spinning a web. One animal after another invites the spider to engage in other activities, but the spider is not distracted from her work. As I read to my daughter, I imitated the voice of each animal—for example, reading the cow's words in a deep, slow, and slurred sort of voice: "Moo!" said the cow. "Want to eat some grass?" In contrast, I read the other words in a typical read-aloud voice, such as the refrain, "The spider didn't answer. She was very busy spinning her web."

As I read each animal voice, my daughter erupted in peals of laughter. Once each animal voice was over, her laughter subsided and she would turn her head to look expectantly to the right—the spot from which I would turn the page and begin another animal voice. Although only 6 months old, my daughter was already beginning to comprehend the story's pattern, its purpose (to entertain), and its power (to make Mommy sound funny!).

While the term *comprehension* may lead us to think of older children and school tests and exercises, as this anecdote reveals, comprehension development begins in infancy, if not before, and is part of meaningful interactions that happen every day in homes, communities, and educational settings.

Young children can be powerful text comprehenders. We do not expect children to be able to read written texts independently from birth to age 5, but we can work to develop children's ability to understand texts that are read aloud to them (*listening comprehension*). In the preschool years, from ages 3 to 5, educators also work to develop children's ability to understand stories and information presented in videos, such as PBS KIDS programs (*viewing comprehension*). Children's listening and viewing comprehension, along with other knowledge and skills, build the foundation for their ability to comprehend printed texts they are able to read independently later on. This process may occur in one named language—for example, English—or across named languages as young children draw on their full communicative repertoires.

Young children start to make meaning and make sense of the world around them from infancy, as they recognize an adult's voice and associate it with comfort and as they associate places (such as a rocking chair) with nourishment. Later, they start "reading" and comprehending the world around them. They comprehend, for example, that the green iron structures on New York City sidewalks show them where to enter to go underground and ride the subway (Souto-Manning & Yoon 2018). Therefore, young children are comprehenders long before they start reading printed texts.

KEY PRACTICES

Knowing and Showing

The key practice of **Knowing** is a starting point for supporting children's development of comprehension skills. **Showing**, another key practice, is the active response to Knowing.

Knowing

Reading aloud to young children offers a variety of benefits and is a recommended practice from birth. Through read alouds, young children are introduced to different worlds and ideas that go beyond the here and now. They are also introduced to the language of texts, which can be quite different from the everyday language we use in speech. Written language often uses different words and sentence structures than we use in our everyday conversations (see Chapter 1). By reading aloud to young children from a variety of texts, teachers can support the development of children's language and comprehension skills.

It's important to go beyond simply reading the words on a page. Educators can also interact with young children while reading. Research shows that the talk that occurs in addition to reading the words on the page supports language and literacy development in preschool-age children (Cabell et al. 2019; Zucker et al. 2013). Discussions are important during read alouds. These discussions can happen before, during, and after the read aloud. Teachers might explain vocabulary words to children to help them understand the text. They might ask open-ended *why* and *how* questions that require higher-level thinking and abstract language (*inferential language*). They might draw children's attention to print features on a page. These conversations allow teachers to scaffold young children's language and knowledge (Zucker et al. 2021). Teachers might repeat, expand, and extend children's language and ideas. All the while, teachers ensure that these discussions enhance, rather than interfere with, children's understanding of the text.

The genre and features of the texts themselves can influence what teachers and children might talk about. For example, while reading a storybook, a teacher might focus on elements, such as the

KEY IDEA

Different Read Alouds Serve Different Purposes

Throughout this book, we have discussed different types of read alouds, each with a different purpose, focus, and invitation for ways children can respond to the text.

- In Chapter 1, we discussed read alouds to support children's **vocabulary and knowledge development.** Children have opportunities to think and learn about new words and ideas.
- In Chapter 2, we talked about read alouds that **reference print.** Children have opportunities to learn about how print works.
- In Chapter 3, we talked about books that **play with sounds in words** and alphabet books to support children's understandings that words can be broken into sounds and that sounds can be represented by letters.
- In Chapter 4, we discussed making books with children and reading them to bring **texts with children's own words** into the classroom.
- In this chapter, we describe ways to use read alouds to develop children's ability to comprehend written language.

No matter how teachers help children learn during read alouds, they can engage children in interacting around the texts—talking, thinking, pointing, acting, and using the ideas they discover in texts.

characters, setting, problem, attempts to solve the problem, and resolution. On the other hand, while reading an informational text, a teacher might focus on the content knowledge children are learning from the text. Teachers might draw attention to structural features that help children find and learn that content, such as the table of contents or glossary. They might also compare and contrast concepts to scaffold children's understanding of the content (Price, Bradley, & Smith 2012).

The Importance of Informational Texts

It is important to keep in mind that although informational texts have traditionally been used less often in early childhood settings, they are developmentally appropriate for young children. Consider this excerpt from a Head Start classroom during a read aloud of an information book about how ice cream is made:

Reader: He has a freezer suit on.

Kenny: Why?

Althea: Cause he won't, cause he can't get cold.

Kenny: Cause he won't catch a cold.

Jason: Yeah, and not get a cough. (Tower 2002, 72)

This discussion about a book reveals that young children can be powerful comprehenders of informational text. Children are piecing together information from the words and pictures in a book, along with their own knowledge, to engage in a complex mental activity called *inferencing*. They have inferred the reason the worker is wearing a special suit—for protection from the cold. The children have also demonstrated the ability to construct meaning together by having a conversation regarding the content of a book.

Showing

When you observe adults and older children reading, they are typically quiet and still. But inside their minds, there's a beehive of activity. Skilled readers' minds are highly active, a storm of synapses as they work to construct meaning and respond to what they are reading.

As early childhood educators, it is important to know about some of the common mental activities associated with successful comprehension so you can "think aloud" about those activities. Thinking aloud is an important way of showing young children what is going on inside the brains of readers. It models and encourages children's use of those mental activities while they are listening to texts read aloud. The table that follows overviews several mental activities that skilled readers engage in and examples for how educators can think aloud. Later in their development, children will practice these mental activities when they read books themselves.

Mental Activity	Goal of the Activity	Thinking Aloud with Infants and Young Toddlers	Thinking Aloud with Older Toddlers and Preschoolers
Skilled readers set goals for their reading.	Think about the purpose or goals for reading.	"Let's find a book to help you feel better."	"We need to find a book that tells us what to feed the cricket."
Skilled readers consider the purpose of the text.	Consider the reason(s) for which a text was written.	"These books have songs we can sing."	"This recipe explains how to cook tamales."
Skilled readers preview what they are about to read.	Examine a text before reading it to note what it is and how it might be organized. (Some call this a *picture walk*, but there's more than pictures to comprehend in texts.)	"I see a lot of pictures of giraffes in this book. I know you love giraffes!"	"I see the author has written the names of different parts of animals' bodies."
Skilled readers make predictions.	Make predictions during reading about what might happen next or what the author might tell us next.	"I think it will be a sunny day in the story next."	"The author told us what dolphins eat. Now I think they will tell us what whales eat."

Table 5.1. Thinking Aloud to Show the Mental Activities of Skilled Readers

(Note: Some of the content in this table comes from Duke et al. 2011 and The Great First Eight Infant and Toddler Curriculum Development Team 2022.)

Mental Activity	Goal of the Activity	Thinking Aloud with Infants and Young Toddlers	Thinking Aloud with Older Toddlers and Preschoolers
Skilled readers integrate background knowledge.	Think about what one knows related to the text.	"Look at his feet. Here are your feet."	"That's a train. It travels underground, just like the train you use to see your grandpa."
Skilled readers make inferences.	Use one's background knowledge and what the text says or shows in pictures to figure out something not explicitly stated in the text.	"I think she is feeling sad. She dropped her ice cream and her face looks sad."	"I think the plants were smaller because it didn't rain much. They didn't get much water."
Skilled readers ask questions.	Wonder about something related to the text.	"I wonder what kind of flower that will be."	"I wonder why pangolins curl up like that."
Skilled readers monitor comprehension.	Pay attention to whether what is being read makes sense and, if not, do something to address the problem.	"Oops, I missed a page. I'll go back."	"Wait—that didn't make sense! I'll read that again."
Skilled readers can retell a story.	Tell, act out, fingerplay, or otherwise retell a version of a story (usually shortened) from memory.	"In this story, a child fell down and scraped their knee. But they were okay."	"In this story, a little girl walked into the woods until . . ."
Skilled readers summarize information.	Identify what the book was about and some key points learned.	"This was a book about playing peekaboo."	"We learned that worms help the earth in many ways."

Table 5.1. Thinking Aloud to Show the Mental Activities of Skilled Readers (continued)

TEACHING TIP

Reading with Expression

Reading with a lot of variation in your voice to match what is in the book (or other text) helps children comprehend its meaning. For example, if the character in the story is frightened, make your voice sound frightened. If a fact is unbelievable, state it with great emphasis and a tone of amazement.

You can also use gestures when reading. For example, knock on a door when a character in the text does so, or use your hands to show how large a particular animal is in real life.

Show How to Engage in Discussions About Text

Toddlers and preschoolers are not too young to have substantive discussions about the books that adults read aloud. It is a common misconception that children should sit quietly and learn to be "good listeners" while adults read aloud. Studies with young learners show that engaging children in talk during read alouds is critical for their learning (National Early Literacy Panel 2008). The goal of educators is to support young children in thinking and talking about texts. This means that you help young learners learn *how* to participate in discussions of text. This is not something that can happen in one day. Like anything else that children learn, this is something to work on over time.

How can educators help young children learn to engage in discussions?

- **Start with a small group of children.** It's a lot easier for children to wait to speak while two or three other children talk compared to waiting for a whole class of children.
- **In whole group discussions, don't expect to call on every child for every question**. Use think-pair-share to provide more children with an opportunity to speak and listen. For simple questions, consider inviting choral and gestural responses (such as thumbs up/down).
- **Make a clear plan for how children show that they want a chance to speak.** For example, the teacher can facilitate discussions by giving children a special object or toy that the speaker holds to show that it is their turn to speak.
- **Ask open-ended questions so that there are a lot of opportunities for children to contribute.** For example, "What is the name of the child in the story?" has one correct answer, so only one child can respond. If you instead ask questions like "How do you think the child in the story is feeling right now?" and "Why do you think that?" then there can be a lot of possible responses.
- **Use nonverbal response techniques.** Not all children feel comfortable responding verbally to a text. Consider inviting children to respond in ways that use movement (for example, performing an action demonstrated in the book) or facial expressions (for example, "How do you think you would feel if this happened to you? Show me with your face").
- **Give children time to think.** It can be hard for children to think of exactly what they want to say right away. Consider giving children some time to think about what they want to say or to turn and talk to just one other child about their ideas before inviting them to share with a larger group.
- **Have children plan for discussion by drawing or writing about their ideas**. Invite children to think about an important idea about a text or multiple texts (for example, "What did you learn from reading this book?") and draw or write about their ideas. Have children bring their work to a group discussion to show and tell their thoughts.
- **Use sentence starters.** Chapter 1 includes a list of sentence starters to help children begin to share their ideas. These work well for discussions about texts. Remember that sentence starters should not be used to correct children's language if they are already participating in a discussion. Rather, these are scaffolds that can be offered to support children who may not feel comfortable participating because they are not sure what to say or how to say it.
- **Teach children to listen and "add on."** When a teacher tries to facilitate a discussion with young children, the conversation can sometimes feel very disjointed when each child's idea is unrelated to what the previous speaker has said. Invite children to listen carefully and add on to another child's ideas. It might be helpful to repeat what the previous child has said (for example, "Gaelen said that the boy in the story feels proud. Isla, do you want to add on to that idea?").

KEY PRACTICES

Designing and Including

Designing as a key practice includes the intentional planning and preparation of the classroom, schedule, and materials to provide a rich variety of learning experiences. **Including** is a key practice essential to ensuring that every child experiences belonging and is welcomed to all learning experiences, ensuring equal access to learning, and fostering respectful and affirming relationships.

Designing

Young children learn as they engage with different types of texts, including texts in different formats and with a variety of features (Neuman & Wright 2007).

Infants. Board books, soft vinyl books, and cloth books are easier for infants to play with and manipulate. They enjoy looking at books with large, prominent pictures that stand out against a contrasting background. Often these books will show just one picture on each page. Choose books about familiar subjects with images of children and babies, toys, foods, or animals. Also, choose books that prompt the reader to make noises (bark like a dog or cluck like a chicken). Finally, choose books that represent Black, Indigenous, and other characters and authors of color. These allow infants to see themselves, their families, and their communities in books and classroom materials as well as to learn about people from other backgrounds. While infants notice and pay attention when readers make surprising or unfamiliar sounds, they also attend to familiar expressions and words that may be used at home (Souto-Manning et al. 2021). For example, an infant in a family that speaks Spanish will likely attend to the reading of a board book that includes the word *hola* for *hello*.

Recommended Types of Books for Infants:

- Board books
- Vinyl or cloth books
- Books with large, prominent pictures
- Books with one picture on each page

Young toddlers. Many toddlers still enjoy board books, but they also enjoy books with standard bindings. Toddlers particularly love books that they can manipulate, such as lift-the-flap books, pop-up books, and books that make noises. The more surprising and sillier the book, the more engaged toddlers are likely to be!

Look for books about concepts that toddlers find interesting, such as books about animals, trains, trucks, parts of the body, or families. Choose many books for toddlers that have characters or images of families and settings that represent their own identities as well as the broader community around them.

During read alouds, toddlers like to help to say words for images they know. Some toddlers may invent unique words for images. For example, coauthor Mariana Souto-Manning's son Thomas always said *água* for *water* (favoring the word in Portuguese) and *buxy* for *coffee* (his shortened version of Starbucks). We note this as it is important for educators to comprehend children's communicative practices instead of seeking to intervene without further observation. In addition, choose some books that children can help read aloud. For example, consider using rhyming books and inviting toddlers to chant along or fill in the words that they know.

Recommended Types of Books for Young Toddlers:

- Concept books, such as books about trucks or paletas
- Rhyming books
- Books children can manipulate (lift-the-flap books, pop-up books)
- Books that represent familiar settings, people, and experiences (for example, young toddlers in New York City are more likely to be familiar with subways than those in Columbia, South Carolina)

Older toddlers and preschoolers. Children who are 2 or 3 years old enjoy storybooks as well as books that provide information about topics of interest. Books with few words on each page and illustrations that support the information in the text help toddlers and young preschoolers to engage with stories and information. Older preschoolers often enjoy longer narratives or books with a lot of facts and information. They can begin to think and talk about stories with more abstract concepts (such as friendship or kindness) and learn about places and ideas that are beyond their immediate experiences.

Toddlers and preschoolers also love books that play with the sounds of language. They often ask their teachers and family members to read favorite books again and again and chant along as adults read. Children of this age also enjoy alphabet books that pair the letter symbols with images of words that start with that letter (more on alphabet books in Chapter 3). Be sure to take the classroom community's language practices in consideration especially if the children you serve have language practices that are unfamiliar to you.

Recommended Types of Books for Older Toddlers and Preschoolers:

- Storybooks (introducing more complex narratives and describing abstract ideas as children get older)
- Informational books (introducing more complex information about new or unfamiliar experiences as children get older)
- Mixed-genre books (with both storybook and informational book elements)
- Books that play with sounds in language (including rhyming, but also features, such as alliteration)
- Alphabet books (in the languages of the classroom community)
- Multilingual books or books that portray multilingualism and translanguaging (especially if there are multilingual children and families in the classroom and/or broader community)

Including

To include all children and communicate belonging, it is important for children to see themselves in books. At the same time, children also benefit from being exposed to unfamiliar language, family, and community practices. The book *Grandma's Records*, by Eric Velasquez, introduces the experience of spending the summer away from parents and with his abuela (grandmother) in Spanish Harlem, learning all about her favorite salsa records. (Both *salsa* and *records* may be unfamiliar to some young children.) *Octopus Stew*, also by Eric Velasquez, employs language practices that draw on vocabulary across the named languages of English and Spanish and uses expressions like *¡Tenga cuidado!* that may be unfamiliar to some children while familiar to others. *Octopus Stew* has a glossary of terms with a pronunciation guide, which explains that *Wela* (short for *abuela*) is the author's name for his grandma and *pulpo guisado* is octopus stew. It also includes an octopus stew recipe (Eric's dad's!).

Work toward diversity, equity, and inclusion in read alouds by considering books as mirrors, windows, and sliding glass doors, as described in the following sections (Bishop 1990).

Mirrors

Having books as mirrors means choosing books with authors and illustrators that reflect children's backgrounds and in which children can find themselves. This is especially important for Black children, Indigenous children, and other children of color given the overwhelming majority of books by White authors and illustrators and with White characters. This is illustrated in Figure 5.1, which shows that there are more children's books depicting characters that are animals and trucks than books depicting characters who are people of color.

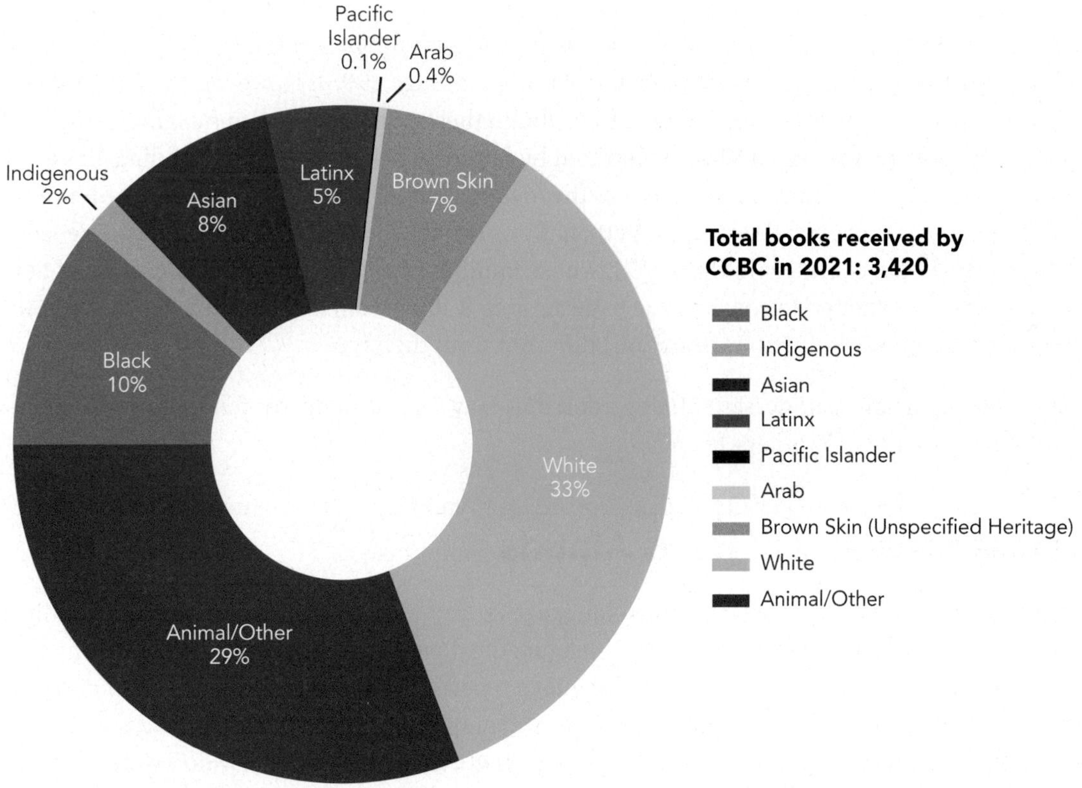

Figure 5.1. This graph shows apparent racial representation of characters in children's books.

Created by Erikson Institute based on data compiled by the Cooperative Children's Book Center, School of Education, University of Wisconsin-Madison (CCBC), on books by and about Black people, Indigenous people, and other people of color published for children and teens (https://ccbc.education.wisc.edu/literature-resources/ccbc-diversity-statistics/books-by-and-or-about-poc-2018).

Having a book as a mirror means that instead of simply choosing a counting book that features animals or robots, you might choose a book like Yuyi Morales's *Just a Minute: A Trickster Tale and Counting Book*, which allows Latinx children to find themselves in a counting book. Or instead of selecting an alphabet book that you treasured as a child, you can purposefully select a book like Yuyi Morales's *Just In Case: A Trickster Tale and Spanish Alphabet Book*.

Windows

Books also serve as windows, so that young children can look through and see unfamiliar images, experiences, identities, and language practices. As windows, books allow young children to consider and learn about experiences, language practices, and identities that differ from their own—an experience that all children need. In addition to providing diverse texts in the classroom, teachers communicate that "diverse perspectives and experiences are truly valued and valuable" (Enriquez 2021, 106).

Sliding Glass Doors

Finally, when books serve as sliding glass doors, they allow children to go beyond the window and imagine entering that unfamiliar world. Books that serve as sliding glass doors invite children to learn about new experiences, language practices, and identities. Actively engaging children in experiences that expand their understandings is at the core of what we have come to know as *culturally relevant teaching* (Ladson-Billings 1995). However, to help children enter other worlds, educators need to help to facilitate these opportunities. For example, the book *Big Red Lollipop*, by Rukhsana Khan, illustrated by Sophie Blackall, may offer a sliding glass door for young children, introducing them to the idea that siblings may be expected to attend birthday parties, even when they are not personally or directly invited. Through the experience of Rubina (the main character in this book), whose family's expectations differ from those of her peers, children are invited to consider the expectations Rubina's family has, allowing children to potentially enter a world (or an expectation) different from theirs.

(Note: It is important to understand that a book that may serve as a mirror for some children may be a sliding glass door for others.)

Translanguaging in Read Alouds

Books that translanguage, or weave named languages together, are more likely to reflect multilingual children's practices. Books that include translanguaging do not separate languages according to adult conventions; they demonstrate a full language repertoire to communicate. In Carmen Tafolla's *What Can You Do with a Paleta?*, there are several examples of translanguaging. The phrases "the smell of crispy tacos or buttery tortillas or juicy *fruta* floats out of every window" and "where the paleta wagon rings its tinkly bell and carries a treasure of icy *paletas* in every color of the *sarape*" both employ translanguaging. So does the book *Round Is a Tortilla: A Book of Shapes*, by Roseanne Thong, illustrated by John Parra (for example, "Round are *sombreros*" and "Round are *campanas* that chime and ring"). The very title of the book *Besos for Baby: A Little Book of Kisses*, by Jen Arena, illustrated by Blanca Gómez, is in itself an example of translanguaging.

KEY IDEA

Selecting Storybooks for Read Alouds

When selecting storybooks for read alouds, consider these four questions:

1. **Who are the characters?** Consider the characters' racial and ethnic identities as well as their language and cultural practices in light of your classroom community and the characters of books you already have.
2. **What is the story?** Is this a story that may be seen as stereotypical; for example, are all of the books in your classroom about Latinx people focused on crossing the border? Are all of the books featuring Black characters about Rev. Dr. Martin Luther King Jr., the civil rights movement, or other historical events?
3. **Who are the author(s) and illustrator(s)?** How do their backgrounds and identities impact the story or information being presented? How do contexts, funds of knowledge, and experiences presented by the author(s) and/or illustrator(s) reflect and/or extend children's contexts and experiences, therefore supporting comprehension? For example, a child familiar with a tortilla will be more likely to understand the concept of round in the book *Round Is a Tortilla: A Book of Shapes.*
4. **What language practices and varieties are featured?** Is this a book in English only? What kinds of language varieties are present? Given multilingual young children do not separate languages, translanguaging is recommended for the earliest years. If you do not speak the language featured in a given book, try learning its key phrases, common expressions, and important words and/or ask a family or community member to read it.

These questions draw our attention not only to the characters featured in books but also to the stories that are told.

Songs, rhymes, and stories in the classroom should not be restricted by the boundaries of English, Spanish, Chinese, Arabic, or any other named language. Instead, they should bring named languages together, illustrating and affirming translanguaging. After all, translanguaging more accurately reflects young children's communicative processes.

In addition to read alouds, other kinds of media like television shows and films support children's learning. For example, the television series *Ada Twist, Scientist* supports children's understandings about the role of Black women in science, and *Hair Love* is a short film that counters misunderstandings about hair.

Take the time to learn about books and other media that are family favorites as well. Invite families to share stories orally or read books, always remembering to ask the four questions discussed earlier.

When you think about children's comprehension development, you need to think about what children are asked to comprehend. Children have a right to comprehend texts that are written by, are illustrated by, and feature people that mirror their identities, languages, and cultural practices.

RECOMMENDED RESOURCES

Children's Books

Infants and Toddlers

- *Baby Goes to Market*, by Atinuke, illustrated by Angela Brooksbank
- *Besos for Baby: A Little Book of Kisses*, by Jen Arena, illustrated by Blanca Gómez
- *Cool Cuts*, by Mechal Renee Roe
- *Every Little Thing*, adapted by Cedella Marley, illustrated by Vanessa Brantley-Newton
- *Happy Hair*, by Mechal Renee Roe
- *Little You*, by Richard Van Camp, illustrated by Julie Flett
- *Sonrisas for Baby: A Little Book of Smiles*, by Jen Arena, illustrated by Blanca Gómez
- *Tickle, Tickle*, by Dakari Hru, illustrated by Ken Wilson-Max

Preschoolers

- *Drawn Together*, by Minh Lê, illustrated by Dan Santat
- *Bedtime Bonnet*, by Nancy Redd, illustrated by Nneka Myers
- *Little Night/Nochecita*, by Yuyi Morales
- *Lucía the Luchadora*, by Cynthia Leonor Garza, illustrated by Alyssa Bermudez
- *Niño Wrestles the World*, by Yuyi Morales
- *Señor Pancho Had a Rancho*, by René Colato Laínez, illustrated by Elwood Smith
- *We Are Grateful: Otsaliheliga*, by Traci Sorell, illustrated by Frané Lessac
- *What Can You Do with a Paleta?* by Carmen Tafolla, illustrated by Magaly Morales

Furthermore, children have a right to comprehend texts that feature voices, images, and people who are new to them. Careful consideration of the books put in front of children is an important part of your role as an early childhood educator.

Children's literacy development needs to prioritize children's rights. This means prioritizing respect for the child's family and community, their cultural identity, language practices, and values, even when these may differ from those of the dominant culture in the community, city, state, or country in which you live. To do this, teachers need to

- Consider what prior information and experiences children may have that will facilitate their comprehension
- Select books that do not reflect bias or racism (Gardner-Neblett et al. 2022)
- Make sure their book choices reflect the images, values, experiences, and language practices of young children as well as provide windows into new and unfamiliar ones

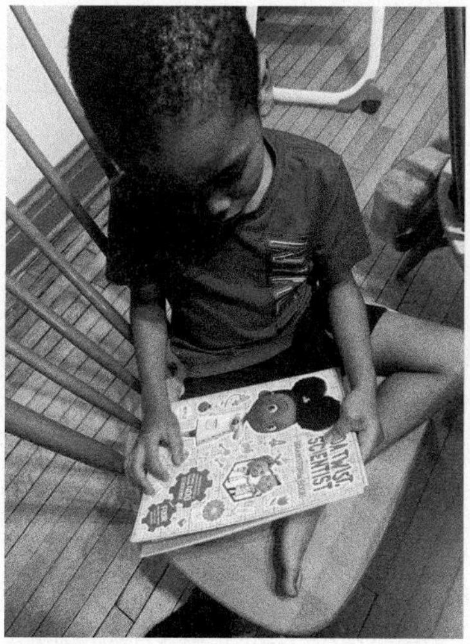

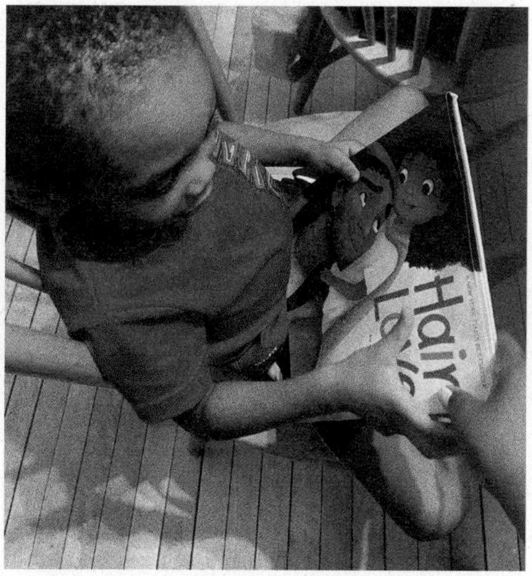

Figures 5.2 and 5.3. Books and other media that have positive representations of children of color are important to supporting children's development.

KEY PRACTICES

Engaging and Explaining

Engaging children in text comprehension is a key practice that happens throughout the day during planned activities, daily routines, and play. Through the key teaching practice of **Explaining**, teachers provide important support for learning to comprehend text.

Engaging

Families and community members can play an essential role in designing and implementing literacy activities that are engaging to children and foster inclusion. Including all families and communities is important because the knowledge, practices, values, and histories of communities of color have been marginalized in curriculum and excluded from teaching (Souto-Manning & Martell 2016; Templeton & Cheruvu 2020).

Engaging with families and community members can help foster inclusive early childhood classrooms by addressing the overrepresentation of White characters in commercial (trade) children's books. Families and community members can recommend, preview, and suggest topics for books. Learning from families and community members is necessary for inclusion and can help educators identify and avoid practices that are misinformed by stereotypes of dominant narratives within racial, ethnic, and cultural groups (Bell 2007; Ramsey 2004; Sue, Neville, & Smith 2019).

Funds of Knowledge

Families have knowledge that can make classrooms more inclusive. Young children bring with them knowledge and practices developed in their families and communities, and educators can build on this knowledge and these practices in teaching and learning. This is particularly relevant in comprehension, given the importance of experience, context, and prior knowledge to comprehension.

KEY IDEA

Document Families' Funds of Knowledge

A trusting relationship between school and home is essential before accessing a family's funds of knowledge. As explained in previous chapters, funds of knowledge are "historically accumulated and culturally developed bodies of knowledge and skills essential for household or individual functioning and well-being" (Moll et al. 1992, 133). Sharing funds of knowledge is an effective way to connect homes and classrooms (Moll et al. 1992). A valuable resource for documenting funds of knowledge as a starting point is a tool developed by Bank Street College of Education that identifies funds of knowledge in alignment with the Head Start framework.

Name: ______________________ Date: __________

Funds of Knowledge	
Home Language	*E.g., Arabic; Spanish; Navajo; Italian*
Family Values and Traditions	*E.g., holiday celebrations; religious beliefs; work ethic*
Caregiving	*E.g., swaddling baby; giving baby pacifer; co-sleeping*
Friends and Family	*E.g., visiting grandma; barbecues; sports outings*
Family Outings	*E.g., shopping; beach; library; picnic*
Household Chores	*E.g., sweeping; dusting; doing dishes*
Educational Activities	*E.g., going to the museum; taking a walk in the neighborhood*
Favorite TV Shows	*E.g., watching Dora; Sesame Street; Sid the Science Kid*
Family Occupations	*E.g., fishing; office; construction; policeman*
Scientific Knowledge	*E.g., recycling; exercising; health*
	Additional Funds of Knowledge

Table 5.2. Funds of Knowledge

Reprinted with permission from Bank Street. Adapted by the National Center on Culturally and Linguistically Responsiveness from N. González, L.C. Moll, & C. Amanti, eds., *Funds of Knowledge: Theorizing Practices in Households, Communities, and Classrooms* (Mahwah, NJ: Erlbaum, 2005).

Documenting and learning about families' funds of knowledge are important considerations throughout your classroom, including materials, images, and play areas. For example, during pretend play, you might intentionally and purposefully include props like empty food packages that represent what is eaten at home (Maseca, rice noodles) or bilingual menus from restaurants in the communities (a Dominican restaurant's menu with text in Spanish and English and pictures or a Chinese restaurant's menu with text in Chinese and English). The goal is to provide texts that represent families' funds of knowledge; serve as windows, mirrors, and sliding glass doors; and support the development of text comprehension.

Text-Related Play

Children engage in many types of play related to texts that are read in their homes and classrooms (Rowe 1998). You may observe children

- Reenacting or playing out favorite parts or scenes of books
- Pretending to be a book character in their play or telling an adult or peer to be a book character as part of their play
- Including book actions or book language (such as dialogue or phrases) from books in their play
- Embellishing or adapting ideas from books (such as combining book ideas with their own experiences or ideas)
- Seeking out or holding toys related to books during read alouds (such as wanting to hold a dinosaur toy while reading a book about dinosaurs)
- Making their own props or costumes or setting up a scene from a book (such as moving furniture or telling other children to stand or sit in a certain place)
- Pretending to read or write books as part of their play

All of these behaviors represent children's attempts to make sense of the ideas they learn in texts. They also show children's engagement with texts and should be encouraged and included in early childhood classrooms.

RESEARCH NOTE

Story Acting

Adults can foster children's comprehension of texts by facilitating children's text-related play. In a study with kindergartners, researchers compared children's comprehension of stories with and without the opportunity to act out the story for 10 minutes following the read aloud. For example, after hearing *The Three Little Pigs*, children had the opportunity to play with finger puppets and props related to the story. After hearing *The Three Billy Goats Gruff*, children used furniture and rugs in the classroom to act out the story. The researchers found that children who had the opportunity to engage in text-related play had better comprehension of the stories (Moedt & Holmes 2020; Paley 1997).

Multimodal Interactions with Text

Not all interactions with text need to be verbal responses. Young children can engage with ideas in read alouds through play and other multimodal activities. Young children develop text comprehension as they

- **Create art in the style of a text.** There are so many ways children can create artwork inspired by the texts they read. Explore collages like artist Oge Mora's illustrations, or use dry leaves and make leaf art like author and illustrator Lois Ehlert. Read *Mouse Paint*, by Ellen Stoll Walsh, and then mix paint colors.
- **Sketch during the read aloud.** Inviting children to draw pictures and write symbols related to what they are hearing while they listen to a read aloud is a powerful learning opportunity (Harste, Short, & Burke 1988; Souto-Manning & Martell 2016).
- **Use puppets to act out a text.** Children love to reenact texts with puppets or felt characters. Provide children with puppets (or have children help make puppets with brown paper bags or socks) and invite children to retell a familiar story.
- **Use props related to a text during dramatic play.** In particular, consider props that represent new vocabulary words in the text. For example, after reading about gardening, provide children with different toy vegetables or gardening tools in the dramatic play area. Show children these objects and invite them to use them as part of their play.
- **Dress up and pretend to be characters from a text.** Children may do this without prompting in dramatic play (for example, "I'll be Piggie and you be Elephant"). Educators can also create opportunities by inviting children to act out favorite books or stories (Paley 1997).
- **Apply ideas from a text to a class project.** For example, after learning about museums through a book or other text, children can create their own classroom museum for families and others to visit.
- **Make a picture that shows ideas from a text.** Invite children to draw their thoughts about a text (for example, "Draw something you learned from our reading," "Draw what you felt when you were reading," or "Draw what you pictured on this page").
- **Take photos or make videos that relate to a text.** For example, when reading a book about another community, such as *Abuela*, by Arthur Dorros, illustrated by Elisa Kleven, take a walk around your school neighborhood with digital cameras or iPads/tablets and invite children to take photos of what they see and/or interview people in the community.

Engaging children in text comprehension is enriched when we tap into families' funds of knowledge, encourage text-related play, invite children to act out stories, and provide opportunities to generate multimodal responses to texts.

Explaining

Books read aloud to children almost always require some explanation. For example, Vanessa Brantley-Newton's book *Grandma's Purse* ends with, "And I know what will go in first." Children may need help inferring that what will go in first is the photo of the little girl with Grandma Mimi. They may need help making the connection that Grandma's purse had family photos in the bottom of it, so the little girl wants family photos in the bottom of her purse too. They may also need prompting to understand that family is more important to Grandma Mimi, and the little girl, than any of the things in their purse. You could, for example, point out to children the photos of Grandma Mimi hugging, kissing, laughing, and smiling with her granddaughter and then ask how Grandma Mimi feels about her granddaughter.

Information books often require explanations as well. For example, in Jill McDonald's book *Pets*, children are asked whether they can twitch their nose like a rabbit. This response requires that they understand what *twitch* means. In the same book, children may need help applying the statement that an ant's "body is divided into three parts: a head, a thorax, and abdomen" to the pictures on the page.

TECHNOLOGY TIP

Talk About Videos

Like books, videos for young children often require explanations. Research suggests that educational video has the most positive effect on children when it is co-viewed—that is, when adults watch along with them (Strouse et al. 2018). The opportunity to pause video and discuss or explain what is happening is extremely important to developmentally appropriate use of video.

With both video and written texts, what we need to explain depends on the child or children in front of us. Consider the *Molly of Denali* episode "Berry Itchy Day." In this story, Molly and her family's trip to pick berries is derailed because Molly accidentally brought the dog perfume instead of much-needed mosquito repellant. Molly ends up making insect repellent using ingredients found in the woods. Depending on where children live, they may need an explanation of what mosquitos are. Some children may need help understanding that many things people buy in a store, such as insect repellent, can be homemade. What explanations are needed depends on children's experiences; this is yet another reason why it is important to learn about children and their families and communities.

Figure 5.4. A scene from the *Molly of Denali* episode "Berry Itchy Day."

Printed with permission from WGBH Boston.

Prompts and Explanations

When teachers read to children, they can provide both explanations and prompts to support children's comprehension. As discussed earlier, think alouds describe what's going on in a reader's mind as they read. Teachers can also use prompting and questioning. One way to prompt and question children during read aloud is *dialogic reading*, a practice designed for one-on-one or small group reading with children. Two acronyms for strategies associated with dialogic reading are PEER and CROWD (Whitehurst 2002), and they are explored in more detail in the following table.

These strategies are appropriate for infants, toddlers, and preschoolers. For all ages, you can discuss what you see in a picture (see **O**pen-ended prompts in the table) or you can **E**xpand on or extend the children's response (for example, "A frog—a big, green frog!"). The **D**istancing prompts (that encourage children to connect something in the text to something outside the text) may be

Step	Example(s)
Prompt the child	
Completion prompts: Prompts children to fill in parts of the text that repeat or rhyme	"But ________________" [expecting children to repeat the recurring phrase "there was the mouse!" in the book *A Visitor for Bear*, by Bonny Becker, illustrated by Kady MacDonald Denton] "One, two, buckle my ________"
Recall prompts: Prompts children to recall a text they've just listened to or listened to on a previous day	"What happened when Goldilocks went into the bear's house?" "What did we learn last time we read this book about how some caterpillars change?"
Open-ended prompts: Prompts children to comment on something in the illustrations of a text	"Tell me what's happening in this picture." "What do you notice in this part of the picture?"
Wh- prompts: Prompts children to answer *who, what, when, where, why*, or *how* questions (these can be open ended as well)	"How do you think those children are feeling?" "Why did the ball roll faster that time?"
Distancing prompts: Prompts children to connect something in the text to something outside the text	"When have you felt sad like that?" "What kinds of insects did we see on our walk?"
Evaluate the child's response	"That's right." "I agree!"
Expand on or extend the child's response	Child: "Frog" Adult: "Yes, it says, 'A frog jumps.'" [discussing text from the book *Jump!* by Tatsuhide Matsuoka]
Repeat key learning	"Let's repeat, 'frogs jump!'"

Table 5.3. PEER and CROWD

particularly valuable for infants and young toddlers as they help young children make connections between books and their lives. For example, you might play peekaboo with an infant and then bring out a book about playing peekaboo, such as *Peek-a-You!* by Andrea Pinkney, illustrated by Brian Pinkney. Or you might pull out a rattle the child uses while reading a book with a rattle. Infants tend to rely more on spatial location to learn new words, rather than the social cues that toddlers use (Pruden et al. 2006). This might mean carrying or leading an infant to a location that connects to a book, such as a window. Take some time to think about how you can make connections between books and children's experiences in and outside of the classroom.

TRANSITIONS

Building Text Comprehension During Transitions

Transitions that involve walking and waiting times, such as walking to another part of the building or waiting for a bus, are opportunities to foster comprehension development. Retell a story that you recently read aloud or discuss interesting facts from a recent informational text you read. Connecting previous read alouds, videos, or other media to things you are seeing or hearing—for example, during a walk outside—can also support comprehension development.

KEY PRACTICES

Observing and Responding

Observing children is a key practice that informs teachers' understanding of children's learning—where they are now in their development and what they are ready to learn next. What you learn through observation will guide you in effectively **Responding** to children in ways that support learning.

Observing

Observing children's interactions with, behaviors, and responses to texts informs your teaching because you gain insights about children's interests, experiences, knowledge, and practices. The following are suggestions for the kinds of things you should observe to inform your selection of books for read alouds as well as how you engage with children during read alouds.

Observe children's interest in the book. When children interact with a book individually, do they linger on that book or quickly move to find another? When you read aloud, do they look at the book or look around the room? These observations can help you select books to read, adjust the amount of time you spend on different parts of the text, and decide when to stop reading.

Observe children's actions with the book. Do children attempt to turn to, or back to, a particular part of a book? Do they point to something they notice? These observations can help guide what you read, as you don't always need to read the whole book or even read the pages in order. In addition, these observations will guide how you offer prompts and comments to children, such as "You turned the page!" or "You really love the part where he runs to the door!"

Observe what children say about the book. Do children chime in as you read certain parts of a book? What do their comments reveal about their understanding of the book? Observations like these help you know what to ask about or comment on as you read and inform decisions about what you read aloud next.

Observe what interests children when they're not with a book. This may seem counterintuitive, but what children are doing when not with a book can inform what and how educators read to them. For example, if you notice children taking interest in some birds outside the window, you might read aloud a book about birds. If you notice a child persisting at a task, later during a read aloud, you might point out a character persisting in a story.

Observe and talk with families. Make connections between children's lives at home with their families and their lives in your classrooms. Observe families and engage in conversations with families to identify interests, cultural practices, and experiences that can inform how you select books and other text materials, as well as the ways in which you read them. For example, if you learn that a family celebrates Chinese New Year, you might read the book *Bringing In the New Year*, by Grace Lin.

Responding

Observation informs educators' work with children, supporting their development as text comprehenders. These observations help educators to understand and plan for ways to scaffold learning for young children.

When you observe the child . . .	You may respond by . . .
Infants	
Looking at a page being read.	Continuing to talk about images or reading the text multiple times. Infants will look away when they are no longer interested.
Pointing to pictures.	Naming the picture the child is pointing to. Name the same picture multiple times if the child continues to point.
Babbling in ways that mimic the sound of adult voices when they read.	Encouraging this behavior by reading to the infant often in an expressive voice.
Interacting with interactive elements of books (sounds, touch, mirrors).	Acknowledging and narrating children's actions. "You see the baby in the mirror. That's you! You see Olivia in the mirror. There's Olivia!"

Table 5.4. Observing and Responding

When you observe the child . . .	You may respond by . . .
Infants	
Playing with a book (touching, holding, shaking, banging on, or chewing) or trying to turn pages.	Allowing children to safely engage in exploration of books like other objects in their environment. Infants may interact with books as a type of toy. This is developmentally appropriate.
Toddlers	
Bringing books to adults to read aloud.	Reading the book to the child or inviting the child to put the book in a special place where you can remember to read it as soon as possible.
Using one or two words to name images.	Encouraging the child to name other images on the page or to say more about the image that you are looking at.
Responding to questions that require a one- or two-word answer. For example, "What is that?" (truck) or "Is that a big truck?" (yes or no).	Asking more open-ended questions to which the child can provide a longer response. For example, "What is happening on this page?" or "What do you notice?"
Asking questions ("What is that?").	Answering the question and asking the child whether they have more questions about the book.
Starting to fill in rhyming words or chant along with familiar texts.	Showing appreciation for the child reading aloud with you. Use a pace and cadence that helps children join in. Pause as needed. For example, in *Moo, Ba, La La La!* by Sandra Boynton, stop and let children fill in the animal names or make animal noises.
Preschoolers	
Showing an interest in a particular topic by including it often in play, conversations, or their choice of books and other activities.	Helping the child to pick out books on that topic to look at and read aloud. "Let's find some books about dinosaurs."
Incorporating vocabulary, stories, characters, and other elements from read alouds in their play.	Providing props and costumes children may need to pretend or act out favorite books, such as *Pete's a Pizza*, by William Steig.
Using words, phrases, or ideas from texts in their everyday language.	Acknowledging and encouraging this behavior. "I see that you are using the flashlight to be a firefly, like in the book we read about summertime."
Making connections between their own identities, languages, and cultural practices, as well as experiences and those of characters in the text.	Inviting children to make more connections. For example, in the book *I Can Do It Too!* by Karen Baicker, illustrated by Ken Wilson-Max, a little girl repeats "I can do it too" as her dad pours juice, her grandmother bakes a cake, and the next-door neighbor rides a bike. After reading this book, ask each child what they can do.
Talking about characters in text ("He was being mean" or "She's a nice friend").	Inviting children to say more. "What was he doing that was mean?"
Responding to open-ended questions about the text.	Invite other children to respond as well. Use phrases like "Say more" or "Can you add on?" to help children discuss ideas in the text.

Table 5.4. Observing and Responding (continued)

Moving Forward

Of the areas of literacy development we have addressed in this book, text comprehension may be least likely to come to mind when people think of early childhood literacy development. But as you have seen, there is so much teachers can do to promote text comprehension development long before children can read texts themselves.

Among other things, you foster children's text comprehension development when you

- **Know** the importance of reading aloud and inviting children to engage with a range of types of text and text genres.
- **Show** children how readers think as they read by engaging in think alouds and helping children learn how to engage in discussions about texts.
- **Design** opportunities for children to engage with texts in a variety of ways, such as naming images, answering questions, and discussion, but also in multimodal ways, such as acting out texts as part of dramatic play, making art related to texts, or engaging in meaningful projects.
- **Include** all children in learning by reading aloud from texts that act as mirrors, windows, and sliding glass doors in children's lives and texts that build on families' and communities' funds of knowledge.
- **Engage** children in text-related play, story acting, and multimodal responses to texts.
- **Explain** ideas in written and video texts and use dialogic reading to support text comprehension development.
- **Observe** children's behaviors with and without texts to guide book selection and your support of children's interactions with texts.
- **Respond** to children by validating and encouraging their thinking.

Young children are making sense of their world right from the start! At every age, educators can support children's understanding of texts by engaging in back-and-forth conversations that build and support literacy development. We recommend choosing both storybooks and informational texts, including books that build on the funds of knowledge held by children's families and communities. See what piques children's interests and involve them as active participants as you read aloud throughout the day.

Let's Get Started!

When coauthor Tanya Wright's daughter was a toddler, she asked to "work" on Tanya's laptop. She sat pressing the keys and typing letters on a blank document, concentrating for a surprising amount of time. Eventually, Tanya said, "You are working hard. What are you working on?" Her daughter responded, "I'm writing an emu."

Across the book, we have shared wonderful moments like these because there is nothing more joyful than being part of a child's journey into literacy. Whether it is watching children imitate adults' literacy behaviors (like working on an email), using new words that they've learned (*emu*/*email*), or engaging in behaviors shown in any of the other anecdotes we've shared throughout the book, we hope it is clear that children's early literacy experiences matter!

The practices early childhood educators use are critical for supporting literacy learning opportunities. We hope that you will reflect on the critical practices discussed in each chapter and continually consider whether and to what degree you are using these practices in your classroom. We know that some ideas in this book may be new or different, but teaching is also a journey, and we think now is the right time to take action, get started, and try something new!

References

Bell, L.A. 2016. "Theoretical Foundations for Social Justice Education." In *Teaching for Diversity and Social Justice*, 3rd ed., ed. M. Adams, 21–44. New York: Routledge.

Bishop, R.S. 1990. "Mirrors, Windows, and Sliding Glass Doors." *Perspectives: Choosing and Using Books for the Classroom* 6 (3): ix–xi.

Cabell, S.Q., T.A. Zucker, J. DeCoster, C. Melo, L. Forston, & B. Hamre. 2019. "Pre-Kindergarten Interactive Book Reading and Children's Language and Literacy Development: Classroom Organization as a Moderator." *Early Education and Development* 30: 1–18.

Duke, N.K., P.D. Pearson, S.L. Strachan, & A.K. Billman. 2011. "Essential Elements of Fostering and Teaching Reading Comprehension." In What Research Has to Say About Reading Instruction, 4th ed., ed. S.J. Samuels & A.E. Farstrup, 51–93. Newark, DE: International Reading Association.

Enriquez, G. 2021. "Foggy Mirrors, Tiny Windows, and Heavy Doors: Beyond Diverse Books Toward Meaningful Literacy Instruction." *The Reading Teacher* 75 (1): 103–106.

Gardner-Neblett, N., A. Addie, A.L. Eddie, S.K. Chapman, N.K. Duke, & C.D. Vallotton. 2022. *It Starts Early. Let's Start Now: A Guide to Selecting Anti-Racist and Anti-Bias Books for Infants and Toddlers*. Ann Arbor: University of Michigan.

The Great First Eight Curriculum Development Team. 2022. *The Great First Eight Infant and Toddler Curriculum*. Ann Arbor: Regents of the University of Michigan.

Harste, J., K. Short, & C. Burke. 1988. *Creating Classrooms for Authors: The Reading-Writing Connection*. Portsmouth, NH: Heinemann.

Ladson-Billings, G. 1995. "But That's Just Good Teaching! The Case for Culturally Relevant Pedagogy." *Theory into Practice* 34 (3): 159–65.

Moedt, K., & R.M. Holmes. 2020. "The Effects of Purposeful Play After Shared Storybook Readings on Kindergarten Children's Reading Comprehension, Creativity, and Language Skills and Abilities." *Early Child Development and Care* 190 (6): 839–54.

Moll, L.C., C. Amanti, D. Neff, & N. Gonzalez. 1992. "Funds of Knowledge for Teaching: Using a Qualitative Approach to Connect Homes and Classrooms." *Theory into Practice* 31 (2): 132–41.

National Early Literacy Panel. 2008. *Developing Early Literacy: Report of the National Early Literacy Panel*. Washington, DC: National Center for Family Literacy.

Neuman, S.B., & T.S. Wright. 2007. *A Parent's Guide to Reading with Your Young Child*. New York: Scholastic.

Paley, V.G. 1997. *The Girl with the Brown Crayon: How Children Use Stories to Shape Their Lives*. Cambridge, MA: Harvard University Press.

Price, L.H., B.A. Bradley, & J.M. Smith. 2012. "A Comparison of Preschool Teachers' Talk During Storybook and Information Book Read-Alouds." *Early Childhood Research Quarterly* 27 (3): 426–40.

Pruden, S.M., K. Hirsh-Pasek, R.M. Golinkoff, & E.A. Hennon. 2006. "The Birth of Words: Ten-Month-Olds Learn Words Through Perceptual Salience." *Child Development* 77 (2): 266–80.

Ramsey, P.G. 2004. *Teaching and Learning in a Diverse World: Multicultural Education for Young Children*. New York: Teachers College Press.

Rowe, D.W. 1998. "The Literate Potentials of Book-Related Dramatic Play." *Reading Research Quarterly* 33 (1): 10–35.

Souto-Manning, M., & J. Martell. 2016. *Reading, Writing, and Talk: Inclusive Teaching Strategies for Diverse Learners, K–2*. New York: Teachers College Press.

Souto-Manning, M., J. Martell, A.Y. Pérez, & P. Pión. 2021. "Translanguaging as Norm: Rejecting Narrow and Restrictive Notions of Reading." *The Reading Teacher* 75 (3): 339–50.

Souto-Manning, M., & H.S. Yoon. 2018. *Rethinking Early Literacies*. New York: Routledge.

Strouse, G.A., G.L. Troseth, K.D. O'Doherty, & M.M. Saylor. 2018. "Co-Viewing Supports Toddlers' Word Learning from Contingent and Noncontingent Video." *Journal of Experimental Child Psychology* 166: 310–26.

Sue, D.W., H.A. Neville, & L. Smith. 2019. *Counseling the Culturally Diverse: Theory and Practice*. 8th ed. Hoboken, NJ: John Wiley and Sons.

Templeton, T., & R. Cheruvu. 2020. "Childhood Innocence for Settler Children: Disrupting Colonialism and Innocence in Early Childhood Curriculum." *The New Educator* 16 (2): 1–18.

Tower, C. 2002. "'It's a Snake, You Guys!': The Power of Text Characteristics on Children's Responses to Information Books." *Research in the Teaching of English* 37 (1): 55–88.

Whitehurst, G.J. 2002. "Dialogic Reading: An Effective Way to Read Aloud." *Reading Rockets*. www.readingrockets.org/article/dialogic-reading-effective-way-read-aloud-young-children.

Zucker, T.A., S.Q. Cabell, L.M. Justice, J.M. Pentimonti, & J.N. Kaderavek. 2013. "The Role of Frequent, Interactive Prekindergarten Shared Reading in the Longitudinal Development of Language and Literacy Skills." *Developmental Psychology* 49: 1425–39.

Zucker, T.A., S.Q. Cabell, Y. Petscher, H. Mui, S.H. Landry, & J. Tock. 2021. "Teaching Together: Pilot Study of a Tiered Language and Literacy Intervention with Head Start Teachers and Linguistically Diverse Families." *Early Childhood Research Quarterly* 54: 136–52.

Index

Page numbers followed by *f* and *t* indicate figures and tables, respectively.

R

S

T

U

V

W